# Hitchcock's
# Bible Names
## Dictionary

by
Roswell D Hitchcock

**Aaron:** a teacher; lofty; mountain of strength

**Abaddon:** the destroyer

**Abagtha:** father of the wine-press

**Abana:** made of stone; a building

**Abarim:** passages; passengers

**Abba:** father

**Abda:** a servant; servitude

**Abdeel:** a vapor; a cloud of God

**Abdi:** my servant

**Abdiel:** servant of God

**Abdon:** servant; cloud of judgment

**Abednego:** servant of light; shining

**Abel:** vanity; breath; vapor

**Abel:** a city; mourning

**Abel-beth-maachah:** mourning to the house of Maachah

**Abel-maim:** mourning of waters

**Abel-meholah:** mourning of sickness

**Abel-mizraim:** the mourning of Egyptians

**Abel-shittim:** mourning of thorns

**Abez:** an egg; muddy

**Abi:** my father

**Abiah:** the Lord is my father

**Abi-albon:** most intelligent father

**Abiasaph:** consuming father; gathering

**Abiathar:** excellent father; father of the remnant

**Abib:** green fruit; ears of corn

**Abidah:** father of knowledge

**Abidan:** father of judgment

**Abiel:** God my father

**Abiezer:** father of help

**Abigail:** the father's joy

**Abihail:** the father of strength

**Abihu:** he is my father

**Abihud:** father of praise; confession

**Abijah:** the Lord is my father

**Abijam:** father of the sea

**Abilene:** the father of mourning

**Abimael:** a father sent from God

**Abimelech:**  father of the king

**Abinadab:**  father of a vow, or of willingness

**Abinoam:**  father of beauty

**Abiram:**  high father; father of deceit

**Abishag:**  ignorance of the father

**Abishai:**  the present of my father

**Abishalom:**  father of peace

**Abishua:**  father of salvation

**Abishur:**  father of the wall; father of uprightness

**Abital:**  the father of the dew; or of the shadow

**Abitub:**  father of goodness

**Abiud:**  father of praise

**Abner:**  father of light

**Abram:**  high father

**Abraham:**  father of a great multitude

**Absalom:**  father of peace

**Accad:**  a vessel; pitcher; spark

**Accho:**  close; pressed together

**Aceldama:**  field of blood

**Achab:**  brother of the father

**Achaia:** grief; trouble

**Achaicus:** a native of Achaia; sorrowing; sad

**Achan:** or Achar, he that troubleth

**Achaz:** one that takes, or possesses

**Achbor:** a rat; bruising

**Achim:** preparing; revenging; confirming

**Achish:** thus it is; how is this

**Achmetha:** brother of death

**Achor:** trouble

**Achsah:** adorned; bursting the veil

**Achshaph:** poison; tricks

**Achzib:** liar; lying; one that runs

**Adadah:** testimony of the assembly

**Adah:** an assembly

**Adaiah:** the witness of the Lord

**Adaliah:** one that draws water; poverty; cloud; death

**Adam:** earthy; red

**Adamah:** red earth; of blood

**Adami:** my man; red; earthy; human

**Adar:** high; eminent

**Adbeel:** vapor, or cloud of God

**Addi:** my witness; adorned; prey

**Addin:** adorned; delicious; voluptuous

**Addon:** basis; foundation; the Lord

**Adiel:** the witness of the Lord

**Adin:** Adina, adorned; voluptuous; dainty

**Adithaim:** assemblies; testimonies

**Adlai:** my witness; my ornament

**Admah:** earthy; red; bloody

**Admatha:** a cloud of death; a mortal vapor

**Adna:** pleasure; delight

**Adnah:** eternal rest

**Adoni-bezek:** the lightning of the Lord; the Lord of lightning

**Adonijah:** the Lord is my master

**Adonikam:** the Lord is raised

**Adoniram:** my Lord is most high; Lord of might and elevation

**Adoni-zedek:** justice of the Lord; lord of justice

**Adoraim:** strength of the sea

**Adoram:** their beauty; their power

**Adrammelech:** the cloak, glory, grandeur or power of the king

**Adramyttium:** the court of death

**Adriel:** the flock of God

**Adullam:** their testimony; their prey; their ornament

**Adummim:** earthy; red; bloody things

**Aeneas:** praised; praiseworthy

**Aenon:** a cloud; fountain; his eye

**Agabus:** a locust; the father's joy or feast

**Agag:** roof; upper floor

**Agar:** or Hagar, a stranger; one that fears

**Agee:** a valley; deepness

**Agrippa:** one who causes great pain at his birth

**Agur:** stranger; gathered together

**Ahab:** uncle, or father's brother

**Aharah:** a smiling brother; a meadow of a sweet savor

**Aharhel:** another host; the last sorrow; a brother's sheep

**Ahasbai:** trusting in me; a grown-up brother

**Ahasuerus:** prince; head; chief

**Ahava:** essence; being; generation

**Ahaz:** one that takes or possesses

**Ahaziah:** seizure; vision of the Lord

**Ahi:** my brother; my brethren

**Ahiah:** brother of the Lord

**Ahiam:** mother's brother; brother of a nation

**Ahian:** brother of wine

**Ahiezer:** brother of assistance

**Ahihud:** brother of vanity, or of darkness, or of joy, or of praise; : witty brother

**Ahijah:** same with Ahiah

**Ahikam:** a brother who raises up or avenges

**Ahilud:** a brother born, or begotten

**Ahimaaz:** a brother of the council

**Ahiman:** brother of the right hand

**Ahimelech:** my brother is a king; my king's brother

**Ahimoth:** brother of death

**Ahinadab:** a willing brother; brother of a vow

**Ahinoam:** beauty of the brother; brother of motion

**Ahio:** his brother; his brethren

**Ahira:** brother of iniquity; brother of the shepherd

**Ahiram:** brother of craft, or of protection

**Ahisamach:** brother of strength

**Ahishahur:** brother of the morning or dew; brother of blackness

**Ahishar:** brother of a prince; brother of a song

**Ahithophel:** brother of ruin or folly

7

**Ahitub:**  brother of goodness

**Ahlab:**  made of milk, or of fat; brother of the heart

**Ahlai:**  beseeching; sorrowing; expecting

**Ahoah:**  a live brother; my thorn or thistle

**Aholah:**  his tabernacle; his tent

**Aholiab:**  the tent of the father

**Aholibah:**  my tent, or my tabernacle, in her

**Aholibamah:**  my tabernacle is exalted

**Ahumai:**  a meadow of waters; a brother of waters

**Ahuzam:**  their taking or possessing vision

**Ahuzzah:**  possession; seizing; collecting

**Ai:**  or Hai, mass; heap

**Aiah:**  vulture, raven; an isle; alas, where is it?

**Aiath:**  same as Ai; an hour; eye; fountain

**Aijeleth-Shahar:**  the land of the morning

**Ain:**  same as Aiath

**Ajalon:**  a chain; strength; a stag

**Akkub:**  foot-print; supplanting; crookedness; lewdness

**Akrabbim:**  scorpions

8

**Alammelech:** God is king

**Alemeth:** hiding; youth; worlds; upon the dead

**Alexander:** one who assists men

**Alian:** high

**Alleluia:** praise the Lord

**Allon:** an oak; strong

**Allon-bachuth:** the oak of weeping

**Almodad:** measure of God

**Almon:** hidden

**Almon-diblathaim:** hidden in a cluster of fig trees

**Alpheus:** a thousand; learned; chief

**Alush:** mingling together

**Alvah:** his rising up; his highness

**Amad:** people of witness; a prey

**Amal:** labor; iniquity

**Amalek:** a people that licks up

**Aman:** mother; fear of them

**Amana:** integrity; truth; a nurse

**Amariah:** the Lord says; the integrity of the Lord

**Amasa:** sparing the people

**Amasai:** strong

**Amashai:** the people's gift

**Amashi-ali:** same as Amaziah

**Ami:** mother; fear; people

**Amaziah:** the strength of the Lord

**Aminadab:** same as Amminadab

**Amittai:** true; fearing

**Ammah:** my, or his, people

**Ammi:** same as Ammah

**Ammiel:** the people of God

**Ammihud:** people of praise

**Ammi-nadab:** my people is liberal

**Ammishaddai:** the people of the Almighty; the Almighty is with me

**Ammizabad:** dowry of the people

**Ammon:** a people; the son of my people

**Amnon:** faithful and true; tutor

**Amok:** a valley; a depth

**Amon:** faithful; true

**Amorite:** bitter; a rebel; a babbler

**Amos:** loading; weighty

**Amoz:** strong; robust

**Amplias:** large; extensive

**Amram:** an exalted people; their sheaves; handfuls of corn

**Amraphel:** one that speaks of secrets

**Amzi:** strong, mighty

**Anab:** a grape; a knot

**Anah:** one who answers; afflicted

**Anaharath:** dryness, burning, wrath

**Anak:** a collar; ornament

**Anamim:** a fountain; answer; affliction

**Anammelech:** answer; poverty of the king

**Anani:** a cloud; prophecy; divination

**Ananias:** or Ananiah, the cloud of the Lord

**Anathema:** separated; set apart

**Anathoth:** or Anath, answer; song; poverty

**Andrew:** a strong man

**Andronicus:** a man excelling others

**Anem:** or Anen, an answer; their affliction

**Aner:** answer; song; affliction

**Aniam:** a people; the strength or sorrow of people

**Anim:** answerings; singings; afflicted

**Anna:** gracious; one who gives

**Annas:** one who answers; humble

**Antichrist:** an adversary to Christ

**Antioch:** speedy as a chariot

**Antipas:** for all, or against all

**Antipatris:** for, or against the father

**Antothijah:** answers or songs of the Lord; afflictions

**Anub:** same as Anab

**Apelles:** exclusion; separation

**Apharsathchites:** Apharsites (from a root meaning) dividing or rending

**Aphek:** Aphekah, Aphik, strength; a rapid torrent

**Aphiah:** speaking, blowing

**Apocalypse:** uncovering, revelation

**Apocrypha:** hidden

**Apollonia:** perdition, destruction

**Apollonius:** destroying

**Apollos:** one who destroys; destroyer

**Apollyon:** a destroyer

**Appaim:** face; nostrils

**Apphia:** productive; fruitful

**Aquila:** an eagle

12

**Ar:** awakening; uncovering

**Ara:** cursing; seeing

**Arab:** multiplying; sowing sedition; a window; a locust

**Arabia:** evening; desert; ravens

**Arad:** a wild ass; a dragon

**Arah:** the way; a traveler

**Aram:** highness, magnificence, one that deceives; curse

**Aran:** an ark; their curse

**Ararat:** the curse of trembling

**Araunah:** ark; song; joyful cry

**Arba:** four

**Archelaus:** the prince of the people

**Archippus:** a master of horses

**Arcturus:** a gathering together

**Ard:** one that commands; he that descends

**Ardon:** ruling; a judgment of malediction

**Areli:** the light or vision of God

**Areopagus:** the hill of Mars

**Aretas:** agreeable, virtuous

**Argob:** a turf, or fat land

**Ariel:** altar; light or lion of God

**Arimathea:** a lion dead to the Lord

**Arioch:** long; great; tall

**Aristarchus:** the best prince

**Aristobulus:** a good counselor

**Armageddon:** hill of fruits; mountain of Megiddo

**Arnon:** rejoicing; sunlight

**Aroer:** heath; tamarisk

**Arpad:** the light of redemption

**Arphaxad:** a healer; a releaser

**Artaxerxes:** the silence of light; fervent to spoil

**Artemas:** whole, sound

**Arumah:** high; exalted

**Asa:** physician; cure

**Asahel:** creature of God

**Asaiah:** the Lord hath wrought

**Asaph:** who gathers together

**Asareel:** the beatitude of God

**Asenath:** peril; misfortune

**Ashan:** smoke

**Ashbel:** an old fire

14

**Ashdod:** effusion; inclination; theft

**Asher:** happiness

**Ashima:** crime; offense

**Ashkenaz:** a fire that spreads

**Ashnah:** change

**Ashriel:** same as Asareel

**Ashtaroth:** Ashtoreth, flocks; sheep; riches

**Ashur:** who is happy; or walks; or looks

**Asia:** muddy; boggy

**Asiel:** the work of God

**Askelon:** weight; balance; fire of infamy

**Asnapper:** unhappiness; increase of danger

**Asriel:** help of God

**Assir:** prisoner; fettered

**Asshurim:** liers in want; beholders

**Assos:** approaching; coming near

**Assur:** same as Ashur

**Assyria:** country of Assur or Ashur

**Asuppim:** gatherings

**Asyncritus:** incomparable

**Atad:** a thorn

**Atarah:** a crown

**Ataroth:** crowns

**Ataroth-addar:** crowns of power

**Ater:** left hand; shut

**Athach:** thy time

**Athaiah:** the Lord's time

**Athaliah:** the time of the Lord

**Athlai:** my hour or time

**Attai:** same as Athlai

**Attalia:** that increases or sends

**Attalus:** increased, nourished

**Augustus:** increased, augmented

**Ava:** or Ivah, iniquity

**Aven:** iniquity; force; riches; sorrow

**Avim:** wicked or perverse men

**Avith:** wicked, perverse

**Azaliah:** near the Lord

**Azaniah:** hearing the Lord; the Lord's weapons

**Azareel:** help of God

**Azariah:** he that hears the Lord

**Azaz:** strong one

**Azazel:** the scape-goat

**Azaziah:** strength of the Lord

**Azekah:** strength of walls

**Azgad:** a strong army; a gang of robbers

**Azmaveth:** strong death; a he-goat

**Azmon:** bone of a bone; our strength

**Aznoth-tabor:** the ears of Tabor; the ears of purity or contrition

**Azor:** a helper; a court

**Azotus:** the same as Ashdod

**Azriel:** same as Asriel

**Azrikam:** help, revenging

**Azubah:** forsaken

**Azur:** he that assists or is assisted

**Azzan:** their strength

**Azzur:** same as Azur


**Baal:** master; lord

**Baalah:** her idol; she that is governed or subdued; a spouse

**Baalath:** a rejoicing; our proud lord

**Baalath-beer:** subjected pit

17

**Baal-berith:** idol of the covenant

**Baale:** same as Baalath

**Baal-gad:** idol of fortune or felicity

**Baal-hamon:** who rules a crowd

**Baal-hermon:** possessor of destruction or of a thing cursed

**Baali:** my idol; lord over me

**Baalim:** idols; masters; false gods

**Baalis:** a rejoicing; a proud lord

**Baal-meon:** idol or master of the house

**Baal-peor:** master of the opening

**Baal-perazim:** god of divisions

**Baal-shalisha:** the god that presides over three; the third idol

**Baal-tamar:** master of the palm-tree

**Baal-zebub:** god of the fly

**Baal-zephon:** the idol or possession of the north; hidden; secret

**Baanah:** in the answer; in affliction

**Baara:** a flame; purging

**Baaseiah:** in making; in pressing together

**Baasha:** he that seeks, or lays waste

**Babel:** confusion; mixture

**Babylon:** same as Babel

**Baca:** a mulberry-tree

**Bahurim:** choice; warlike; valiant

**Bajith:** a house

**Balaam:** the ancient of the people; the destruction of the people

**Baladan:** one without judgment

**Balak:** who lays waste or destroys

**Bamah:** an eminence or high place

**Barabbas:** son of shame, confusion

**Barachel:** that bows before God

**Barachias:** same as Barachel

**Barak:** thunder, or in vain

**Barjesus:** son of Jesus or Joshua

**Barjona:** son of a Jona; of a dove

**Barnabas:** son of the prophet, or of consolation

**Barsabas:** son of return; son of rest

**Bartholomew:** a son that suspends the waters

**Bartimeus:** son of the honorable

**Baruch:** who is blessed

**Barzillai:** son of contempt; made of iron

**Bashan:** in the tooth, in ivory

**Bashemath:** perfumed; confusion of death; in desolation

**Bathsheba:** the seventh daughter; the daughter of satiety

**Bathsuha:** same as Bathsheba

**Bealiah:** the god of an idol; in an assembly

**Bealoth:** cast under

**Bebai:** void, empty

**Becher:** first begotten; first fruits

**Bechorath:** first fruits

**Bedad:** alone; solitary

**Bedaiah:** Bedeiah, the only Lord

**Bedan:** according to judgment

**Beeliada:** an open idol

**Beelzebub:** same as Baalzebub

**Beer:** a well

**Beera:** a well; declaring

**Beerelim:** the well of Elim, or of rains

**Beeri:** my well

**Beer-lahai-roi:** the well of him that liveth and seeth me

**Beeroth:** wells; explaining

**Beersheba:** the well of an oath; the seventh well

**Behemoth:** beasts

**Bekah:** half a shekel

**Belah:** destroying

**Belial:** wicked, worthless

**Belshazzar:** master of the treasure

**Belteshazzar:** who lays up treasures in secret

**Ben:** a son

**Benaiah:** son of the Lord

**Ben-ammi:** son of my people

**Beneberak:** sons of lightning

**Bene-jaakan:** sons of sorrow

**Benhadad:** son of Hadad, or noise

**Benhail:** son of strength

**Benhanan:** son of grace

**Benjamin:** son of the right hand

**Benimi:** our sons

**Beno:** his son

**Benoni:** son of my sorrow, or pain

**Benzoheth:** son of separation

**Beon:** in affliction

**Beor:** burning; foolish; mad

**Bera:** a well; declaring

**Berachah:** blessing; bending the knee

**Berachiah:** speaking well of the Lord

**Beraiah:** the choosing of the Lord

**Berea:** heavy; weighty

**Bered:** hail

**Beri:** my son; my corn

**Beriah:** in fellowship; in envy

**Berith:** covenant

**Bernice:** one that brings victory

**Berodach-baladan:** the son of death

**Berothai:** wells; a cypress

**Berothath:** of a well

**Besai:** a despising; dirty

**Besodeiah:** counsel of the Lord

**Besor:** glad news; incarnation

**Betah:** confidence

**Beten:** belly

**Bethabara:** the house of confidence

**Bethanath:** house of affliction

**Bethany:** the house of song; the house of affliction

**Betharabah:** house of sweet smell

**Beth-aram:** house of height

**Beth-aven:** the house of vanity; of iniquity of trouble

**Beth-azmaveth:** house of death's strength

**Beth-baalmeon:** an idol of the dwelling-place

**Beth-barah:** the chosen house

**Beth-birei:** the house of my Creator, the house of my health

**Beth-car:** the house of the lamb

**Beth-dagon:** the house of corn, or of fish

**Beth-diblathaim:** house of dry figs

**Beth-el:** the house of God

**Bethemek:** house of deepness

**Bether:** division, or in the trial

**Bethesda:** house of pity or mercy

**Beth-ezal:** a neighbor's house

**Beth-gader:** a house for a mouse

**Beth-gamul:** house of recompense, or of the camel

**Beth-haccerem:** house of the vineyard

**Beth-haran:** house of grace

**Beth-horon:** house of wrath

**Beth-lebaoth:** house of lionesses

**Beth-lehem:** house of bread

**Beth-marcaboth:** house of bitterness wiped out

**Beth-meon:** house of the dwelling-place

**Beth-nimrah:** house of rebellion

**Beth-palet:** house of expulsion

**Beth-pazzez:** house of dividing asunder

**Beth-peor:** house of gaping, or opening

**Bethphage:** house of my month, or of early figs

**Beth-phelet:** same as Beth-palet

**Beth-rapha:** house of health

**Bethsaida:** house of fruits, or of food, or of snares

**Bethshan:** Beth-shean, house of the tooth, or of ivory, or of sleep

**Beth-shemesh:** house of the sun

**Bethuel:** filiation of God

**Beth-zur:** house of a rock

**Betonim:** bellies

**Beulah:** married

**Bezai:** eggs

**Bezaleel:** in the shadow of God

**Bezek:** lightning; in the chains

**Bezer:** vine branches

**Bichri:** first-born; first fruits

**Bidkar:** in compunction, or sharp pain

**Bigthan:** in the press; giving meat

**Bigvai:** in my body

**Bildad:** old friendship

**Bileam:** the ancient of the people; the devourer

**Bilgah:** ancient countenance

**Bilhah:** Bilhan, who is old or confused

**Bilshan:** in the tongue

**Binea:** son of the Lord

**Binnui:** building

**Birsha:** an evil; a son who beholds

**Bishlam:** in peace

**Bithiah:** daughter of the Lord

**Bithron:** divisions

**Bithynia:** violent precipitation

**Bizjothjah:** despite

**Blastus:** that buds or brings forth

**Boanerges:** son of thunder

**Boaz:** or Booz, in strength

**Bocheru:** the first born

**Bochim:** the place of weeping; or of mulberry-trees

**Bohan:** in them

**Boskath:** in poverty

**Boson:** taking away

**Bozez:** mud; bog

**Bozrah:** in tribulation or distress

**Bukki:** void

**Bukkiah:** the dissipation of the Lord

**Bul:** old age; perishing

**Bunah:** building; understanding

**Bunni:** building me

**Buz:** despised; plundered

**Buzi:** my contempt

**Cabbon:** as though understanding

**Cabul:** displeasing; dirty

**Caiphas:** he that seeks with diligence; one that vomiteth

**Cain:** possession, or possessed

**Cainan:** possessor; purchaser

26

**Calah:** favorable; opportunity

**Calcol:** nourishing

**Caleb:** a dog; a crow; a basket

**Caleb-Ephratah:** see Ephratah

**Calneh:** our consummation

**Calno:** our consummation; altogether himself

**Calvary:** the place of a skull

**Camon:** his resurrection

**Cana:** zeal; jealousy; possession

**Canaan:** merchant; trader; or that humbles and subdues

**Candace:** who possesses contrition

**Capernaum:** the field of repentance; city of comfort

**Caphtor:** a sphere, buckle, or hand

**Cappadocia:** the same as Caphtor

**Carcas:** the covering of a lamb

**Charchemish:** a lamb; as taken away; withdrawn

**Careah:** bald; ice

**Carmel:** circumcised lamb; harvest; full of ears of corn

**Carmi:** my vineyard; lamb of the waters

**Carpus:** fruit; fruitful

**Carshena:** a lamb; sleeping

**Casiphia:** money; covetousness

**Casluhim:** hopes of life

**Cedron:** black; sad

**Cenchrea:** millet; small pulse

**Cephas:** a rock or stone

**Cesar:** a name applied to those who are cut out of the womb

**Chalcol:** who nourishes, consumes, and sustains the whole

**Chaldea:** as demons, or as robbers

**Charran:** a singing or calling out

**Chebar:** force or strength

**Chedorlaomer:** roundness of a sheaf

**Chelal:** as night

**Chelub:** a basket

**Chelluh:** all

**Chelubai:** he altogether against me

**Chemarims:** black ones

**Chemosh:** handling; stroking; taking away

**Chenaanah:** broken in pieces

**Chenani:** my pillar

**Chenaniah:** preparation, or disposition, or strength, of the Lord

**Chephirah:** a little lioness

**Cheran:** anger

**Cherethims:** Cherethites, who cut or tear away

**Cherith:** cutting; piercing; slaying

**Chesed:** as a devil, or a destroyer

**Chesil:** foolishness

**Chesulloth:** fearfulness

**Chidon:** a dart

**Chiliab:** totality; or the perfection of the father

**Chilion:** finished; complete; perfect

**Chilmad:** teaching or learning

**Chimham:** as they; like to them

**Chios:** open; opening

**Chisleu :** Cisleu, Casleu, rashness; confidence

**Chislon:** hope, trust

**Chisloth-tabor:** fears; purity

**Chittem:** those that bruise; gold

**Chloe:** green herb

**Chorazin:** the secret; here is a mystery

**Chozeba:** men liers in wait

**Christ:** anointed

**Chun:** making ready

**Chushan-rishathaim:** blackness of iniquities

**Chuza:** the seer or prophet

**Cilicia:** which rolls or overturns

**Cis:** same as Kish

**Clauda:** a lamentable voice

**Claudia** Claudius, lame

**Clement:** mild; good; merciful

**Cleophas:** the whole glory

**Cnidus:** age

**Colhozeh:** every prophet

**Colosse:** punishment; correction

**Coniah:** strength of the Lord

**Coos:** top, summit

**Corinth:** which is satisfied; ornament; beauty

**Cornelius:** of a horn

**Cosam:** divining

**Coz:** a thorn

**Cozbi:** a liar; sliding away

**Crescens:** growing; increasing

**Crete:** carnal; fleshly

**Crispus:** curled

**Cush:** Cushan, Cushi, Ethiopians; blackness

**Cuth:** Cuthah, burning

**Cyprus:** fair; fairness

**Cyrene:** a wall; coldness; the floor

**Cyrenius:** who governs

**Cyrus:** as miserable; as heir

**Dabareh:** the word; the thing; a bee; obedient

**Dabbasheth:** flowing with honey

**Daberath:** same as Dabareh

**Dagon:** corn; a fish

**Dalaiah:** the poor of the Lord

**Dalmanutha:** a bucket; a branch

**Dalmatia:** deceitful lamps; vain brightness

**Dalphon:** the house of caves

**Damaris:** a little woman

**Damascus:** a sack full of blood; the similitude of burning

**Dan:** judgment; he that judges

**Daniel:** judgment of God; God my judge

**Dannah:** judging

**Darah:** generation; house of the shepherd or of the companion

**Darda:** home of knowledge

**Darius:** he that informs himself

**Darkon:** of generation; of possession

**Dathan:** laws or rites

**David:** well-beloved, dear

**Debir:** an orator; a word

**Deborah:** word; thing; a bee

**Decapolis:** containing ten cities

**Dedan:** their breasts; friendship; a judge

**Dedanim:** the descendants of Dedan

**Dekar:** force

**Delaiah:** the poor of the Lord

**Delilah:** poor; small; head of hair

**Demas:** popular

**Demetrius:** belonging to corn, or to Ceres

**Derbe:** a sting

**Deuel:** the knowledge of God

**Deuteronomy:** repetition of the law

**Diana:** luminous, perfect

**Diblaim:** cluster of figs

**Diblath:** paste of dry figs

**Dibon:** abundance of knowledge

**Dibon-gad:** great understanding; abundance of sons

**Dibri:** an orator

**Dibzahab:** Dizahab, where much gold is

**Didymus:** a twin; double

**Diklah:** Dildah, his diminishing

**Dilean:** that is poor

**Dimon:** where it is red

**Dimonah:** dunghill

**Dinah:** judgment; who judges

**Dinhabah:** he gives judgment

**Dionysius:** divinely touched

**Diotrephes:** nourished by Jupiter

**Dishan:** a threshing

**Dishon:** fatness; ashes

**Dodai:** Dodanim, beloved

**Dodavah:** love

**Dodo:** his uncle

**Doeg:** careful, who acts with uneasiness

**Dophkah:** a knocking

**Dor:** generation, habitation

**Dorcas:** a female roe-deer

**Dothan:** the law; custom

**Drusilla:** watered by the dew

**Dumali:** silence; resemblance

**Dura:** same as Dor


**Ebal:** ancient heaps

**Ebed:** a servant; laborer

**Ebed-melech:** the king's servant

**Eben-ezer:** the stone of help

**Eber:** one that passes; anger

**Ebiasaph:** a father that gathers or adds

**Ebronah:** passage over; being angry

**Ecclesiastes:** a preacher

**Ed:** witness

**Eden:** pleasure; delight

**Eder:** a flock

**Edom:** red, earthy; of blood

**Edrei:** a very great mass, or cloud

**Eglah:** heifer; chariot; round

**Eglaim:** drops of the sea

**Eglon:** same as Eglah

**Egypt:** that troubles or oppresses; anguish

**Ehud:** he that praises

**Eker:** barren, feeble

**Ekron:** barrenness; torn away

**Eladah:** the eternity of God

**Elah:** an oak; a curse; perjury

**Elam:** a young man; a virgin; a secret

**Elasah:** the doings of God

**Elath:** a hind; strength; an oak

**El-beth-el:** the God of Bethel

**Eldaah:** knowledge of God

**Eldad:** favored of God; love of God

**Elead:** witness of God

**Elealeh:** burnt-offering of God

**Eleazar:** help of God, court of God

**El-elohe-Israel:** God, the God of Israel

**Eleph:** learning

**Elhanan:** grace, or gift, or mercy of God

**Eli:** the offering or lifting up

**Eli:** Eli, my God, my God

**Eliab:** God is my father; God is the father

**Eliada:** knowledge of God

**Eliah:** God the Lord

**Eliahba:** my God the Father

**Eliakim:** resurrection of God

**Eliam:** the people of God

**Elias:** same as Elijah

**Eliasaph:** the Lord increaseth

**Eliashib:** the God of conversion

**Eliathah:** thou art my God

**Elidad:** beloved of God

**Eliel:** God, my God

**Elienai:** the God of my eyes

**Eliezer:** help, or court, of my God

**Elihoreph:** god of winter, or of youth

**Elihu:** he is my God himself

**Elijah:** God the Lord, the strong Lord

**Elika:** pelican of God

**Elim:** the rams; the strong; stags

**Elimelech:** my God is king

**Elioenai:** toward him are mine eyes; or to him are my fountains

**Eliphal:** a miracle of God

**Eliphalet:** the God of deliverance

**Eliphaz:** the endeavor of God

**Elisabeth:** the oath, or fullness, of God

**Elisha:** salvation of God

**Elishah:** it is God; the lamb of God: God that gives help

**Elishama:** God hearing

**Elishaphat:** my God judgeth

**Elisheba:** same as Elisabeth

**Elishua:** God is my salvation

**Eliud:** God is my praise

**Elizur:** God is my strength; my rock; rock of God

**Elkanah:** God the zealous; the zeal of God

**Elkeshai:** hardiness or rigor of God

**Ellasar:** revolting from God

**Elkoshite:** a man of Elkeshai

**Elmodam:** the God of measure, or of the garment

**Elnaam:** God's fairness

**Elnathan:** God hath given; the gift of God

**Elohi:** Elohim, God

**Elon:** oak; grove; strong

**Elon-beth-hanan:** the house of grace or mercy

**Elpaal:** God's work

**Elpalet:** same as Eliphalet

**Eltekeh:** of grace or mercy

**Elteketh:** the case of God

**Eltolad:** the generation of God

**Elul:** cry or outcry

**Eluzai:** God is my strength

**Elymas:** a magician, a corrupter

**Elzabad:** the dowry of God

**Elzaphan:** God of the northeast wind

**Emims:** fears; terrors; formidable; people

**Emmanuel:** God with us

**Emmaus:** people despised or obscure

**Emmor:** an ass

**Enam:** fountain, open place

**Enan:** cloud

**En-dor:** fountain, eye of generation, or of habitation

**Eneas:** laudable

**En-eglaim:** eye, or fountain, of calves

**En-gannim:** eye, or fountain, of protection or of gardens

**En-gedi:** eye, or fountain, of the goat, or of happiness

**En-haddah:** quick sight; well of gladness

**En-hakkore:** fountain of him that called or prayed

**En-hazor:** the grass of the well

**En-mishpat:** fountain of judgment

**Enoch:** dedicated; disciplined

**Enon:** cloud; mass of darkness; fountain; eye

**Enos:** mortal man; sick; despaired of; forgetful

**En-rimmon:** well of weight

**En-rogel:** the fuller's fountain; the well of searching

**En-shemesh:** fountain, or eye, of the sun

**En-tappuah:** fountain of an apple, or of inflation

**Epaphras:** covered with foam

**Epaphroditus:** agreeable; handsome

**Epenetus:** laudable; worthy of praise

**Ephah:** weary; tired

**Epher:** dust; lead

**Ephes-dammim:** effusion of blood

**Ephesus:** desirable

**Eph-lal:** judging; praying

**Ephphatha:** be opened

**Ephraim:** fruitful; increasing

**Ephratah:** Ephrath, abundance; bearing fruit

**Ephron:** dust

**Epicurean:** follower of Epicurus, i.e., of one who gives assistance

**Er:** watchman

**Eran:** follower

**Erastus:** lovely, amiable

**Erech:** length; health; physic

**Eri:** my city

**Esaias:** same as Isaiah

**Esar-haddon:** that closes the point; joy; cheerfulness

**Esau:** he that acts or finishes

**Esek:** contention

**Esh-baal:** the fire of the idol, or of the ruler

**Esh-ban:** fire of the sun

**Eshcol:** bunch of grapes

**Eshean:** held up

**Eshek:** violence, force

**Eshkalon:** same as Askelon

**Eshtaol:** a strong woman

**Eshtemoa:** the bosom of a woman

**Esli:** near me; he who separates

**Esmachiah:** joined to the Lord

**Esrom:** dart of joy; division of a song

**Esther:** secret; hidden

**Etam:** their bird, their covering

**Etham:** their strength; their sign

**Ethan:** strong; the gift of the island

**Ethanim:** strong; valiant

**Ethbaal:** toward the idol, or with Baal

**Ether:** talk

**Ethiopia:** blackness; heat

**Ethnan:** gift

**Ethni:** strong

**Eubulus:** prudent; good counselor

**Eunice:** good victory

**Euodias:** sweet scent

**Euphrates:** that makes fruitful

**Eutychus:** happy; fortunate

**Eve:** living; enlivening

**Evi:** unjust

**Evil-merodach:** the fool of Merodach; the fool grinds bitterly

**Exodus:** going out, departure

**Ezbon:** hastening to understand

**Ezekiel:** the strength of God

**Ezel:** going abroad; walk

**Ezem:** a bone

**Ezer:** a help

**Ezion-geber:** the wood of the man

**Ezra:** help; court

**Ezri:** my help


**Felix:** happy, prosperous

**Festus:** festive, joyful

**Fortunatus:** lucky, fortunate


**Gaal:** contempt; abomination

**Gaash:** tempest; commotion

**Gabbai:** the back

**Gabbatha:** high; elevated

**Gabriel:** God is my strength

**Gad:** a band; a troop

**Gadarenes:** men of Gadara, i.e., a place surrounded or walled

**Gaddi:** my troop; a kid

**Gaddiel:** goat of God; the Lord my happiness

**Gaius:** lord; an earthly man

**Galal:** a roll, a wheel

**Galatia:** white; the color of milk

**Galeed:** the heap of witness

**Galilee:** wheel; revolution

**Gallim:** who heap up; who cover

**Gallio:** who sucks, or lives on milk

**Gamaliel:** recompense of God; camel of God

**Gammadims:** dwarfs

**Gamul:** a recompense

**Gareb:** a scab

**Garmites:** men of Garmi, ie., bones, or, my cause

**Gatam:** their lowing; their touch

**Gath:** a wine-press

**Gath-rimmon:** the high wine-press

**Gaza:** strong; a goat

**Gazabar:** a treasurer

**Gazer:** a dividing; a sentence

**Gazez:** a passing over

**Gazzam:** the fleece of them

**Geba:** a hill; cup

**Gebal:** bound; limit

**Geber:** manly, strong

**Gebim:** grasshoppers; height

**Gedaliah:** God is my greatness

**Geder:** Gederah, Gederoth, a wall

**Gederothaim:** hedges

**Gehazi:** valley of sight

**Geliloth:** rolling, wheel, heap

**Gemalli:** wares; a camel

**Gemariah:** accomplishment or perfection of the Lord

**Gennesaret:** garden of the prince

**Genesis:** beginning

**Genubath:** theft; robbery

**Gera:** pilgrimage, combat; dispute

**Gerar:** same as Gera

**Gergesenes:** those who come from pilgrimage or fight

**Gerizim:** cutters, hatchets

**Gershom:** a stranger here

**Gershon:** his banishment; the change of pilgrimage

**Geshur:** Geshuri, sight of the valley; a walled valley

**Gether:** the vale of trial or searching

**Gethsemane:** a very fat or plentiful vale

**Geuel:** God's redemption

**Gezer:** dividing, sentence

**Giah:** to guide; draw out; produce; a groan or sigh

**Gibbar:** strong, manly

**Gibbethon:** a back; a high house

**Gibeah:** a hill

**Gibeon:** hill; cup; thing lifted up

**Giddel:** great

**Gideon:** he that bruises or breaks; a destroyer

**Gideoni:** same as Gideon

**Gihon:** valley of grace

**Gilalai:** a wheel

**Gilboa:** revolution of inquiry

**Gilead:** the heap or mass of testimony

**Gilgal:** wheel; rolling; heap

**Giloh:** he that rejoices; he that overturns

**Gimzo:** that bulrush

**Ginath:** Ginnetho, a garden

**Girgashite:** who arrives from pilgrimage

**Gispa:** coming hither

**Gittah-hepher:** digging; a wine-press

**Gittaim:** a wine-press

**Gittites:** men of Gath, ie., of a wine-press

**Goath:** his touching; his roaring

**Gob:** cistern; grasshopper

**Gog:** roof; covering

**Golan:** passage; revolution

**Golgotha:** a heap of skulls; something skull-shaped

**Goliath:** passage; revolution; heap

**Gomer:** to finish; complete

**Gomorrah:** rebellious people

**Goshen:** approaching; drawing near

**Gozan:** fleece; pasture; who nourisheth the body

**Gudgodah:** happiness

**Guni:** a garden; a covering

**Gur:** the young of a beast; a whelp

**Gur-baal:** the governor's whelp


**Haahashtari:** a runner

**Habaiah:** the hiding of the Lord

**Habakkuk:** he that embraces; a wrestler

**Habazinaiah:** a hiding of the shield of the Lord

**Habor:** a partaker; a companion

**Hachaliah:** who waits for the Lord

**Hachilah:** my hope is in her

**Hachmoni:** a wise man

**Hadad:** joy; noise; clamor

**Hadadezer:** beauty of assistance

**Hadadrimmon:** invocation to the god Rimmon

**Hadar:** power; greatness

**Hadarezer:** same as Hadadezer

**Hadashah:** news; a month

**Hadassah:** a myrtle; joy

**Hadid:** rejoicing; sharp

**Hadlai:** loitering; hindering

**Hadoram:** their beauty; their power

**Hadrach:** point; joy of tenderness

**Hagab:** Hagabah, a grasshopper

**Hagar:** a stranger; one that fears

**Haggai:** feast; solemnity

**Haggeri:** Haggi, a stranger

**Haggiah:** the Lord's feast

**Haggith:** rejoicing

**Hakkatan:** little

**Hakkoz:** a thorn; summer; an end

**Hakupha:** a commandment of the mouth

**Halah:** a moist table

**Halak:** part

**Halhul:** grief; looking for grief

**Hali:** sickness; a beginning; a precious stone

**Hallelujah:** praise the Lord

**Halloesh:** saying nothing; an enchanter

48

**Ham:** hot; heat; brown

**Haman:** noise; tumult

**Hamath:** anger; heat; a wall

**Hamath-zobah:** the heat, or the wall, of an army

**Hammedatha:** he that troubles the law

**Hammelech:** a king; a counselor

**Hammon:** heat; the sun

**Hamonah:** his multitude; his uproar

**Hamon-gog:** the multitude of Gog

**Hamor:** an ass; clay; dirt

**Hamoth:** indignation

**Hamul:** godly; merciful

**Hamutal:** the shadow of his heat

**Hanameel:** the grace that comes from God; gift of God

**Hanan:** full of grace

**Hananeel:** grace, or gift, of God

**Hanani:** my grace; my mercy

**Hananiah:** grace; mercy; gift of the Lord

**Hanes:** banishment of grace

**Haniel:** the gift of God

**Hannah:** gracious; merciful; he that gives

**Hannathon:** the gift of grace

**Hanniel:** grace or mercy of God

**Hanoch:** dedicated

**Hanun:** gracious; merciful

**Hapharaim:** searching; digging

**Hara:** a hill; showing forth

**Haradah:** well of great fear

**Haran:** mountainous country

**Harran:** see Charran

**Harbonah:** his destruction; his sword

**Hareph:** winter; reproach

**Harhas:** anger; heat of confidence

**Harhaiah:** heat, or anger, of the Lord

**Harhur:** made warm

**Harim:** destroyed; dedicated to God

**Harnepher:** the anger of a bull; increasing heat

**Harod:** astonishment; fear

**Harosheth:** a forest; agriculture; workmanship; deafness; silence

**Harsha:** workmanship; a wood

**Harum:** high; throwing down

**Harumaph:** destruction

**Haruphite:** slender; sharp

**Haruz:** careful

**Hasadiah:** the mercy of the Lord

**Hashabiah:** the estimation of the Lord

**Hashabnah:** Hashabniah, the silence of the Lord

**Hashem:** named; a putting to

**Hashub:** esteemed; numbered

**Hashubah:** estimation; thought

**Hashum:** silence; their hasting

**Hashupha:** spent; made base

**Hasrah:** wanting

**Hatach:** he that strikes

**Hathath:** fear

**Hatita:** a bending of sin

**Hattil:** howling for sin

**Hattipha:** robbery

**Hattush:** forsaking sin

**Hauran:** a hole; liberty; whiteness

**Havilah:** that suffers pain; that brings forth

**Havoth-jair:** the villages that enlighten

**Hazael:** that sees God

**Hazaiah:** seeing the Lord

**Hazar-addar:** an imprisoned generation

**Hazarenan:** imprisoned cloud

**Hazargaddah:** imprisoned band

**Hazar-hatticon:** middle village; preparation

**Hazarmaveth:** dwelling of death

**Hazar-shual:** a wolf's house

**Hazar-susah:** or susim, the hay-paunch of a horse

**Hazelelponi:** sorrow of countenance

**Hazeroth:** villages; palaces

**Hazezon-tamar:** drawing near to bitterness

**Hazo:** seeing; prophesying

**Hazor:** court; hay

**Heber:** one that passes; anger

**Hebrews:** descendants of Heber

**Hebron:** society; friendship

**Hegai:** or Hege, meditation; word; groaning; separation

**Helam:** their army; their trouble

**Helbah:** Helbon, milk, fatness

**Heldai:** Heleb, Heled, the world; rustiness

**Helek:** part; portion

**Helem:** dreaming; healing

**Heleph:** changing; passing over

**Helez:** armed; set free

**Heli:** ascending; climbing up

**Helkai:** same as Helek

**Helkath-hazzurim:** the field of strong men, or of rocks

**Helon:** window; grief

**Heman:** their trouble; tumult; much; in great number

**Hen:** grace; quiet; rest

**Hena:** troubling

**Henadad:** grace of the beloved

**Henoch:** same as Enoch

**Hepher:** a digger

**Hephzibah:** my delight is in her

**Heres:** the son; an earthen pot

**Heresh:** a carpenter

**Hermas:** Hermes, Mercury; gain; refuge

**Hermogenes:** begotten of Mercury

**Hermon:** anathema; devoted to destruction

**Herod:** son of a hero

**Herodion:** the song of Juno

**Heshbon:** invention; industry

**Heshmon:** a hasty messenger

**Heth:** trembling; fear

**Hethlon:** a fearful dwelling

**Hezekiah:** strength of the Lord

**Hezer:** Hezir, a bog; converted

**Hezrai:** an entry or vestibule

**Hezron:** the dart of joy; the division of the song

**Hiddai:** a praise; a cry

**Hiddekel:** sharp voice; sound

**Hiel:** God lives; the life of God

**Hierapolis:** holy city

**Higgaion:** meditation; consideration

**Hilen:** a window; grief

**Hilkiah:** God is my portion

**Hillel:** he that praises

**Hinnom:** there they are; their riches

**Hirah:** liberty; anger

**Hiram:** exaltation of life; a destroyer

**Hittite:** one who is broken; who fears

**Hivites:** wicked; wickedness

**Hizkijah:** the strength of the Lord

**Hobab:** favored; beloved

**Hobah:** love; friendship; secrecy

**Hod:** praise; confession

**Hodaiah:** the praise of the Lord

**Hodaviah:** Hodiah, Hodijah, same as Hodaiah

**Hodesh:** a table; news

**Hoglah:** his festival or dance

**Hoham:** woe to them

**Holon:** a window; grief

**Homam:** making an uproar

**Hophin:** he that covers; my fist

**Hor:** who conceives, or shows; a hill

**Horam:** their hill

**Horeb:** desert; solitude; destruction

**Horem:** an offering dedicated to God

**Hor-hagidgad:** the hill of felicity

**Hori:** a prince; freeborn

**Horims:** princes; being angry

**Hormah:** devoted or consecrated to God; utter destruction

**Horonaim:** angers; ragings

**Horonites:** men of anger, or of fury, or of liberty

**Hosah:** trusting

**Hosanna:** save I pray thee; keep; preserve

**Hosea:** Hoshea, savior; safety

**Hoshaiah:** the salvation of the Lord

**Hoshama:** heard; he obeys

**Hotham:** a seal

**Hothir:** excelling; remaining

**Hukkok:** engraver; scribe; lawyer

**Hul:** pain; infirmity

**Huldah:** the world

**Hupham:** their chamber; their bank

**Huppim:** a chamber covered; the sea-shore

**Hur:** liberty; whiteness; hole

**Huram:** their liberty; their whiteness; their hole

**Huri:** being angry; or same as Huram

**Hushah:** hasting; holding peace

**Hushai:** their haste; their sensuality; their silence

**Hushathite:** Hushim, man of haste, or of silence

**Huz:** counsel; woods; fastened

**Huzoth:** streets; populous

**Huzzab:** molten

**Hymeneus:** nuptial; the god of marriage

**Ibhar:** election; he that is chosen

**Ibleam:** ancient people; people decreasing

**Ibneiah:** Ibniah, the building of the Lord; the understanding of the Lord;: son by adoption

**Ibri:** passing over; being angry; being with young

**Ibzan:** father of a target; father of coldness

**Ichabod:** where is the glory? or, no glory

**Iconium:** coming

**Idalah:** the hand of slander, or of cursing

**Idbash:** flowing with honey; the land of destruction

**Iddo:** his band; power; praise

**Idumea:** red; earthy; bloody

**Igal:** redeemed; defiled

**Igeal:** a redeemer; redeemed; defiled

**Igdaliah:** the greatness of the Lord

**Iim:** heaps of Hebrews, or of angry men

**Ije-abarim:** heaps of Hebrews, or of passers over

**Ijon:** look; eye; fountain

**Ikkesh:** forward; wicked

**Illyricum:** joy; rejoicing

**Imlah:** plentitude; circumcision

**Immanuel:** God with us

**Immer:** saying; speaking; a lamb

**Imnah:** same as Jimnah

**Imrah:** a rebel; waxing bitter; changing

**Imri:** speaking; exalting; bitter; a lamb

**India:** praise; law

**Iphedeiah:** redemption of the Lord

**Ir:** watchman; city; vision

**Ira:** watchman; making bare; pouring out

**Irad:** wild ass; heap of empire; dragon

**Iram:** the effusion of them; a high heap

**Iri:** fire; light

**Irijah:** the fear of the Lord

**Irpeel:** the health, medicine, or exulting of God

**Irshemesh:** a city of bondage

**Isaac:** laughter

**Isaiah:** the salvation of the Lord

**Iscah:** he that anoints

**Iscariot:** a man of murder; a hireling

**Ishbak:** who is empty or exhausted

**Ishbi-benob:** respiration; conversion; taking captive

**Ishbosheth:** a man of shame

**Ishi:** salvation

**Ishiah:** it is the Lord

**Ishma:** named; marveling; desolation

**Ishmael:** God that hears

**Ishmaiah:** hearing or obeying the Lord

**Ishmerai:** keeper, or keeping

**Ishod:** a comely man

**Ish-pan:** hid; broken in two

**Ish-tob:** good man

**Ishua:** plainness; equal

**Ishmachiah:** cleaving to the Lord

**Ispah:** a jasper stone

**Israel:** who prevails with God

**Issachar:** reward; recompense

**Isui:** same as Ishuah

**Ithai:** strong; my sign; a plowshare

**Italy:** abounding with calves or heifers

**Ithamar:** island of the palm-tree

**Ithiel:** sign, or coming of God

**Ithmah:** an orphan

**Ithran:** remaining; searching out diligently

**Ithream:** excellence of the people

**Ittah-kazin:** hour, or time, of a prince

**Iturea:** guarded; mountainous

**Ivah:** iniquity

**Izehar:** Izhar, clearness; oil

**Izrahiah:** the Lord ariseth; the clearness of the Lord

**Izri:** fasting; tribulation

**Jaakan:** tribulation; labor

**Jaakobah:** supplanter; deceiver; the heel

**Jaala:** ascending; a little doe or goat

**Jaalam:** hidden; young man; heir

**Jaanai:** answering; afflicting; making poor

**Jaasau:** doing; my doing

**Jaasiel:** God's work

**Jaazaniah:** whom the Lord will hear

**Jaazah:** Jaazar, helper

**Jaaziah:** Jaaziel, the strength of the Lord

**Jabal:** which glides away

**Jabbok:** evacuation; dissipation; wrestling

**Jabesh:** dryness; confusion; shame

**Jabez:** sorrow; trouble

**Jabin:** Jabneh, he that understands; building

**Jabneel:** building of God

**Jachan:** wearing out; oppressing

**Jachin:** he that strengthens and makes steadfast

**Jacob:** that supplants, undermines; the heel

**Jada:** knowing

**Jadau:** his hand; his confession

**Jaddua:** known

**Jael:** he that ascends; a kid

**Jagur:** husbandman; stranger

**Jah:** the everlasting

**Jahaleel:** praising God; light of God

**Jahath:** broken in pieces; descending

**Jahaz:** Jahazah, quarrel; dispute

**Jahaziah:** the vision of the Lord

**Jahaziel:** seeing God

**Jahdiel:** the unity, or sharpness, or revenge, of God

**Jahdo:** I alone; his joy; his sharpness of wit; his newness

**Jahleel:** waiting for, or beseeching, or hope in, God

**Jahmai:** warm; making warm

**Jahzeel:** God hasteth, or divideth

**Jair:** Jairus, my light; who diffuses light

**Jakan:** same as Achan

**Jakim:** rising; confirming; establishing

**Jalon:** tarrying; murmuring

**Jambres:** poverty; bitter; a rebel

**James:** same as Jacob

**Jamin:** right hand; south wind

**Jamlech:** reigning; asking counsel

**Janna:** Jannes, who speaks or answers; afflicted; poor

**Janoah:** Janohah, resting; tarrying; deriving

**Janum:** sleeping

**Japhet:** enlarged; fair; persuading

**Japhia:** enlightening; appearing

**Japhlet:** Japhleti, delivered; banished

**Japho:** fairness; comeliness

**Jarah:** a wood; honeycomb; watching closely

**Jareb:** a revenger

**Jared:** a ruling; commanding; coming down

**Jaresiah:** the bed of the Lord; the Lord hath taken away; poverty

**Jarib:** fighting; chiding; multiplying; avenging

**Jarmuth:** fearing, or seeing, or throwing down, death

**Jarvah:** breathing, or making, a sweet smell

**Jashem:** Jashen, ancient; sleeping

**Jasher:** righteous; upright

**Jashobeam:** the people sitting; or captivity of the people

**Jashub:** a returning; a controversy; a dwelling place

**Jasiel:** the strength of God

**Jason:** he that cures

**Jathniel:** gift of God

**Jattir:** a remnant; excellent

**Javan:** deceiver; one who makes sad

**Jazeel:** strength of God

**Jazer:** assistance; helper

**Jaziz:** brightness; departing

**Jearim:** a leap; woods

**Jeaterai:** searching out

**Jeberechiah:** speaking well of, or kneeling to, the Lord

**Jebus:** treading under foot; manger

**Jebusi:** trodden under foot; mangers

**Jecamiah:** resurrection, or confirmation, or revenge, of the Lord

**Jecoliah:** perfection, or power, of the Lord

**Jeconiah:** preparation, or stability, of the Lord

**Jedaiah:** the hand of the Lord; confessing the Lord

**Jedeiah:** one Lord; the joy of the Lord

**Jediael:** the science, or knowledge, of God

**Jedidah:** well beloved; amiable

**Jedidiah:** beloved of the Lord

**Jediel:** the knowledge, or renewing, of God

**Jeduthun:** his law; giving praise

**Jeezer:** island of help

**Jegar-sahadutha:** heap of witness

**Jehaleleel:** Jehalelel, praising God; clearness of God

**Jehaziel:** same as Jahaziel

**Jehdeiah:** joy together, one Lord

**Jeheiel:** God liveth

**Jehezekel:** strength of God

**Jehiah:** the Lord liveth

**Jehiskiah:** the strength, or taking, of the Lord

**Jehoadah:** passing over; testimony of the Lord

**Jehoaddan:** pleasure, or time, of the Lord

**Jehoahaz:** possession of the Lord

**Jehoash:** fire of the Lord

**Jehohanan:** grace, or mercy, or gift, of the Lord

**Jehoiachin:** preparation, or strength, of the Lord

**Jehoiada:** knowledge of the Lord

**Jehoiakim:** avenging, or establishing, or resurrection, of the Lord

**Jehoiarib:** fighting, or multiplying, of the Lord

**Jehonadab:** Jonadab, free giver; liberality

**Jehonathan:** gift of the Lord; gift of a dove

**Jehoram:** exaltation of the Lord

**Jehoshaphat:** the Lord is judge

**Jehosheba:** fullness, or oath, of the Lord

**Jehoshua:** same as Joshua

**Jehovah:** self-subsisting

**Jehovah-jireh:** the Lord will provide

**Jehovah-nissi:** the Lord my banner

**Jehovah-shalom:** the Lord send peace

**Jehovah-shammah:** the Lord is there

**Jehovah-tsidkenu:** the Lord our righteousness

**Jehozabad:** the Lord's dowry; having a dowry

**Jehozadak:** justice of the Lord

**Jehu:** himself who exists

**Jehubbah:** hiding, binding

**Jehucal:** mighty; perfect; wasted

**Jehud:** Jehudi, praising; conferring

**Jehudijah:** the praise of the Lord

**Jehush:** keeping counsel; fastened

**Jekabzeel:** the congregation of God

**Jekamean:** the people shall arise

**Jekamiah:** establishing, or revenging, of the Lord

**Jekuthiel:** hope, or congregation, of the Lord

**Jemima:** handsome as the day

**Jemuel:** God's day; son of God

**Jephunneh:** he that beholds

**Jerah:** the moon; month; smelling sweet

**Jerahmeel:** the mercy, or the beloved, of God

**Jered:** ruling; coming down

**Jeremai:** my height; throwing forth waters

**Jeremiah:** exaltation of the Lord

**Jeremoth:** eminences; one that fears death

**Jeriah:** fear, or throwing down, of the Lord

**Jerebai:** fighting; chiding; multiplying

**Jericho:** his moon; his month; his sweet smell

**Jeriel:** fear, or vision of God

**Jerijah:** same as Jeriah

**Jerimoth:** he that fears or rejects death

**Jerioth:** kettles; breaking asunder

**Jeroboam:** he that opposes the people

**Jeroham:** high; merciful; beloved

**Jerubbaal:** he that defends Baal, let Baal defend his cause

**Jerubbesheth:** let the idol of confusion defend itself

**Jeruel:** fear, or vision of God

**Jerusalem:** vision of peace

**Jerusha:** banished; possession; inheritance

**Jesaiah:** health, or salvation, of the Lord

**Jeshebeab:** sitting, or captivity, of the father

**Jesher:** right; singing

**Jeshimon:** solitude; desolation

**Jeshishai:** ancient; rejoicing exceedingly

**Jeshohaia:** the Lord pressing; the meditation of God

**Jeshua:** same as Joshua

**Jesiah:** sprinkling of the Lord

**Jesimiel:** naming, or astonishment, of God

**Jesse:** gift; oblation; one who is

**Jesui:** even-tempered; flat country

**Jesus:** savior; deliverer

**Jether:** he that excels

**Jetheth:** giving

**Jethlah:** hanging up; heaping up

**Jethro:** his excellence; his posterity

**Jetur:** order; succession; mountainous

**Jeuel:** God hath taken away; God heaping up

**Jeush:** Jeuz, he that is devoured

**Jew:** same as Judah

**Jezaniah:** nourishment, or weapons, of the Lord

**Jezebel:** chaste

**Jezer:** island of help

**Jeziah:** Jeziel, sprinkling of the Lord

**Jezoar:** clear; white

**Jezrahiah:** the Lord arises; brightness of the Lord

**Jezneel:** seed of God

**Jibsam:** their drought, their confusion

**Jidlaph:** he that distills water

**Jimnah:** right hand; numbering; preparing

**Jiphtah:** opening

**Jiphthael:** God opening

**Joab:** paternity; voluntary

**Joah:** fraternity; brother of the Lord

**Joahaz:** apprehending; possessing; seeing

**Joakim:** rising or establishing of the Lord

**Joanna:** grace or gift of the Lord

**Joash:** who despairs or burns

**Joatham:** same as Jotham

**Job:** he that weeps or cries

**Jobab:** sorrowful, hated

**Jochebed:** glorious; honorable

**Joed:** witnessing; robbing; passing over

**Joel:** he that wills or commands

**Joelah:** lifting up; profiting; taking away slander

**Joezer:** he that aids

**Jogbehah:** an exalting; high

**Jogli:** passing over; turning back; rejoicing

**Joha:** who enlivens or gives life

**Johanan:** who is liberal or merciful

**John:** the grace or mercy of the Lord

**Joiarib:** chiding, or multiplying, of the Lord

**Jokdeam:** crookedness, or burning, of the people

**Jokim:** that made the sun stand still

**Jokmeam:** confirmation, or revenge, of the people

**Jokneam:** possessing, or building up, of the people

**Jokshan:** an offense; hardness; a knocking

**Joktan:** small dispute; contention; disgust

**Jonadab:** who gives liberally

**Jonah:** or Jonas, a dove; he that oppresses; destroyer

70

**Jonan:** a dove; multiplying of the people

**Jonathan:** given of God

**Joppa:** beauty; comeliness

**Jorah:** Jorai, showing; casting forth; a cauldron

**Joram:** to cast; elevated

**Jordan:** the river of judgment

**Jorim:** he that exalts the Lord

**Josabad:** having a dowry

**Josaphat:** same as Jehoshaphat

**Jose:** raised; who pardons

**Joseph:** increase; addition

**Joses:** same as Jose

**Joshah:** being; forgetting; owing

**Joshaviah:** the seat, alteration, or captivity of the Lord

**Joshbekesha:** it is requiring or beseeching

**Joshua:** a savior; a deliverer

**Josiah:** the Lord burns; the fire of the Lord

**Josibiah:** the seat, or captivity of the Lord

**Josiphiah:** increase of the Lord; the Lord's finishing

**Jotham:** the perfection of the Lord

**Jothath:** Jothatha, his goodness

**Jozabad:** same as Josabad

**Jozachar:** remembering; of the male sex

**Jubal:** he that runs; a trumpet

**Jucal:** mighty; perfect

**Judah:** the praise of the Lord; confession

**Judas:** Jude, same as Judah

**Judaea:** Judea, same as Judah

**Judith:** same as Judah

**Julia:** downy; soft and tender hair

**Julius:** same as Julia

**Junia:** youth

**Jupiter:** the father that helpeth

**Jushabhesed:** dwelling-place; change of mercy

**Justus:** just or upright

**Juttah:** turning away


**Kabzeel:** the congregation of God

**Kadesh:** holiness

**Kadesh-barnea:** holiness of an inconstant son

**Kadmiel:** God of antiquity; God of rising

**Kadmonites:** ancients; chiefs

**Kallai:** light; resting by fire; my voice

**Kanah:** of reeds

**Kareah:** bald; ice

**Karkaa:** floor; dissolving coldness

**Karkor:** they rested

**Karnaim:** horns

**Kartah:** calling; meeting

**Kedar:** blackness; sorrow

**Kedemah:** oriental; ancient; first

**Kedemoth:** antiquity; old age

**Kehelahath:** a whole; a congregation

**Keiiah:** she that divides or cuts

**Kelaiah:** voice of the Lord; gathering together

**Kelitah:** same as Kelaiah

**Kemuel:** God hath raised up, or established him

**Kenah:** buying; possession

**Kenan:** buyer; owner

**Kenaz:** this purchase; this lamentation

**Kenites:** possession; purchase; lamentation

**Kenizzites:** possession; purchase

**Keren-happuch:** the horn or child of beauty

**Kerioth:** the cities; the callings

**Keros:** crooked; crookedness

**Keturah:** that makes the incense to fume

**Kezia:** superficies; the angle; cassia

**Keziz:** end; extremity

**Kibroth-hattaavah:** the graves of lust

**Kibzaim:** congregation

**Kidron:** obscure; making black or sad

**Kinah:** same as Kenah

**Kir:** a city; wall; meeting

**Kirharaseth:** Kirharesh, city of the sun; wall of burnt brick

**Kirioth:** same as Kerioth

**Kirjath:** city; vocation; meeting

**Kirjathaim:** the two cities; callings; or meetings

**Kirjath-arba:** city of four; fourth city

**Kirjath-arim:** city of those who watch

**Kirjath-baal:** city of Baal, or of a ruler

**Kirjath-huzoth:** city of streets; populous city

**Kirjath-jearim:** city of woods

**Kirjath-sannah:** city of enmity, or of a blackberry bush

**Kirjath-sepher:** city of letters, or of the book

**Kish:** hard; difficult; straw; for age

**Kishi:** hardness; his gravity; his offense

**Kishion:** hardness; soreness

**Kishon:** hard; sore

**Kithlish:** it is a wall; the company of a lioness

**Kitron:** making sweet; binding together

**Kittim:** breaking; bruising small; gold; coloring

**Koa:** hope; a congregation; a line; a rule

**Kohath:** congregation; wrinkle; bluntness

**Kolariah:** voice of the Lord

**Korah:** baldness; ice; frost

**Kushaiah:** same as Kishi

**Laadah:** to assemble together; to testify; passing over

**Laadan:** for pleasure; devouring; judgment

**Laban:** white; shining; gentle; brittle

**Labana:** the moon; whiteness; frankincense

**Lachish:** who walks, or exists, of himself

75

**Lael:** to God; to the mighty

**Lahad:** praising; to confess

**Lahairoi:** who liveth and seeth me

**Lahmam:** their bread; their war

**Lahmi:** my bread; my war

**Laish:** a lion

**Lamech:** poor; made low

**Laodicea:** just people

**Lapidoth:** enlightened; lamps

**Lasea:** thick; wise

**Lashah:** to call; to anoint

**Lazarus:** assistance of God

**Leah:** weary; tired

**Lebanon:** white, incense

**Lebaoth:** lividness

**Lebbeus:** a man of heart; praising; confessing

**Lebonah:** same as Labana

**Lehabim:** flames; inflamed; swords

**Lehi:** jawbone

**Lekah:** walking; going

**Lemuel:** God with them, or him

**Leshem:** a name; putting; a precious stone

**Letushim:** hammermen; filemen

**Leummim:** countries; without water

**Levi:** associated with him

**Libnah:** white; whiteness

**Libni:** same as Libnah

**Libya:** the heart of the sea; fat

**Linus:** net

**Lo-ammi:** not my people

**Lod:** nativity; generation

**Lois:** better

**Lo-ruhamah:** not having obtained mercy; not pitied

**Lot:** Lotan, wrapt up; hidden; covered; myrrh; rosin

**Lubin:** heart of a man; heart of the sea

**Lucas:** Lucius, luminous; white

**Lucifer:** bringing light

**Lud:** Ludim, same as Lod

**Luhith:** made of boards

**Luke:** luminous; white

**Luz:** separation; departure; an almond

**Lycaonia:** she-wolf

**Lydda:** Lydia, a standing pool

**Lysanias:** that drives away sorrow

**Lysias:** dissolving

**Lysimachus:** scattering the battle

**Lystra:** that dissolves or disperses

**Maachah:** pressed down; worn; fastened

**Maachathi:** broken

**Maadai:** pleasant; testifying

**Maadiah:** pleasantness; the testimony of the Lord

**Maai:** belly; heaping up

**Maale-akrabbim:** ascent of scorpions

**Maarath:** den; making empty; watching

**Maaseiah:** the work of the Lord

**Maasiai:** the defense, or strength, or trust of the Lord

**Maath:** wiping away; breaking; fearing; smiting

**Maaz:** wood; wooden

**Macedonia:** burning; adoration

**Machbenah:** Machbanai, poverty; the smiting of his son

**Machi:** poor; a smiter

**Machir:** selling; knowing

**Machnadebai:** smiter

**Machpelah:** double

**Madai:** a measure; judging; a garment

**Madian:** judgment; striving; covering; chiding

**Madmannah:** measure of a gift; preparation of a garment

**Madon:** a chiding; a garment; his measure

**Magbish:** excelling; height

**Magdala:** tower; greatness

**Magdalene:** a person from Magdala

**Magdiel:** declaring God; chosen fruit of God

**Magog:** covering; roof; dissolving

**Magor-missabib:** fear on every side

**Magpiash:** a body thrust hard together

**Mahalah:** Mahalath, sickness; a company of dancers; a harp

**Mahaleleel:** praising God

**Mahali:** infirmity; a harp; pardon

**Mahanaim:** tents; two fields; two armies

**Mahanehdan:** tents of judgment

**Mahanem:** a comforter

**Maharai:** hasting; a hill; from a hill

**Mahath:** same as Maath

**Mahavites:** declaring a message; marrow

**Mahaz:** an end; ending; growing hope

**Mahazioth:** seeing a sign; seeing a letter

**Maher-shalal-hash-baz:** making speed to the spoil; he hastens to the prey

**Mahlah:** Mahli, Mahlon, same as Mahali

**Makas:** same as Mahaz

**Makheloth:** assemblies; congregations

**Makkedah:** worshiping; burning; raised; crookedness

**Malachi:** my messenger; my angel

**Malcham:** Malchom, their king; their counselor

**Malchiah:** Malchijah, the Lord my king, or my counselor

**Malchiel:** God is my king, or counselor

**Malchus:** my king, kingdom, or counselor

**Maleleel:** same as Mahaleleel

**Mallothi:** fullness; circumcision

**Malluch:** reigning; counseling

**Mammon:** riches

**Mamre:** rebellious; bitter; set with trees

**Manaen:** a comforter; a leader

**Manahethites:** my lady; my prince of rest

**Manasseh:** forgetfulness; he that is forgotten

**Manoah:** rest; a present

**Maon:** house; place of sin

**Mara:** Marah, bitter; bitterness

**Maralah:** sleep; a sacrifice of myrrh; ascension

**Maranatha:** the Lord is coming

**Marcus:** polite; shining

**Mareshah:** from the beginning; an inheritance

**Mark:** same as Marcus

**Maroth:** bitterness

**Marsena:** bitterness of a bramble

**Martha:** who becomes bitter; provoking

**Mary:** same as Miriam

**Mash:** same as Meshech

**Mashal:** a parable; governing

**Masrekah:** whistling; hissing

**Massa:** a burden; prophecy

**Massah:** temptation

**Matred:** wand of government

**Matri:** rain; prison

**Mattan:** Mattana, Mattenai, gifts; rains

**Mattaniah:** gift, or hope, of the Lord

**Mattatha:** his gift

**Mattathias:** the gift of the Lord

**Matthan:** same as Mattan

**Matthanias:** same as Mattaniah

**Matthai:** gift; he that gives

**Matthew:** given; a reward

**Matthias:** Mattithiah, same as Mattathias

**Mazzaroth:** the twelve signs of the zodiac

**Meah:** a hundred cubits

**Mearah:** den; cave; making empty

**Mebunnai:** son; building; understanding

**Mecherath:** selling; knowledge

**Medad:** he that measures; water of love

**Medan:** judgment; process

**Medeba:** waters of grief; waters springing up

**Media:** measure; habit; covering

**Megiddo:** his precious fruit; declaring a message

**Megiddon:** same as Megiddo

**Mehetabel:** how good is God

**Mehida:** a riddle; sharpness of wit

**Mehir:** a reward

**Mehujael:** who proclaims God

**Mehuman:** making an uproar; a multitude

**Mejarkon:** the waters of Jordan

**Mekonah:** a foot of a pillar; provision

**Melatiah:** deliverance of the Lord

**Melchi:** my king; my counsel

**Melchiah:** God is my king

**Melchi-shua:** king of health; magnificent king

**Melchizedek:** king of justice

**Melea:** supplying; supplied

**Melech:** king; counselor

**Melita:** affording honey

**Mellicu:** his kingdom; his counselor

**Melzar:** circumcision of a narrow place, or of a bond

**Memphis:** abode of the good

**Memucan:** impoverished; to prepare; certain; true

**Menahem:** comforter; who conducts them; preparation of heat

**Menan:** numbered; rewarded; prepared

**Mene:** who reckons or is counted

**Meonenim:** charmers, regarders of times

**Mephaath:** appearance, or force, of waters

**Mephibosheth:** out of my mouth proceeds reproach

**Merab:** he that fights or disputes

**Meraioth:** bitterness; rebellious; changing

**Merari:** bitter; to provoke

**Mercurius:** an orator; an interpreter

**Mered:** rebellious, ruling

**Meremoth:** bitterness; myrrh of death

**Meres:** defluxion; imposthume

**Meribah:** dispute; quarrel

**Meribbaal:** he that resists Baal; rebellion

**Merodach:** bitter contrition

**Merodach-baladan:** bitter contrition, without judgment

**Merom:** eminences; elevations

**Meronothite:** my singing; rejoicing; bearing rule

**Meroz:** secret, leanness

**Mesha:** burden; salvation

**Meshach:** that draws with force

**Meshech:** who is drawn by force

**Meshelemiah:** peace, or perfection, of the Lord

**Meshezaheel:** God taking away; the salvation of God

**Meshillamith:** peaceable; perfect; giving again

**Meshullam:** peaceable; perfect; their parables

**Mesobaite:** the Lord's standing-place; a little doe

**Mesopotamia:** between two rivers

**Messiah:** anointed

**Metheg-ammah:** bridle of bondage

**Methusael:** who demands his death

**Methusaleh:** he has sent his death

**Meunim:** dwelling-places; afflicted

**Mezahab:** gilded

**Miamin:** the right hand

**Mibhar:** chosen; youth

**Mibsam:** smelling sweet

**Mibzar:** defending; forbidding; taking away

**Micah:** poor; humble

**Micaiah:** who is like to God?

**Micha:** same as Micaiah

**Michaiah:** Michael, same as Micah

**Michal:** who is perfect?

**Michmach:** he that strikes

**Michmethah:** the gift or death of a striker

**Michri:** selling

**Michtam:** golden psalm

**Middin:** judgment; striving

**Midian:** judgment; covering; habit

**Migdalel:** tower of God

**Migdalgad:** tower compassed about

**Migdol:** a tower

**Migron:** fear; farm; throat

**Mijamin:** right hand

**Mikloth:** little wants; little voices; looking downward

**Minneiah:** possession of the Lord

**Milalai:** circumcision; my talk

**Milcah:** queen

**Milcom:** their king

**Miletum:** red; scarlet

**Millo:** fullness

**Miniamin:** right hand

**Minni:** reckoned; prepared

**Minnith:** same as Minni

**Miriam:** rebellion

**Mishael:** who is asked for or lent

**Mishal:** parables; governing

**Misham:** their savior; taking away

**Misheal:** requiring; lent; pit

**Mishma:** hearing; obeying

**Mishmannah:** fatness; taking away provision

**Mishraites:** spread abroad

**Mispar:** Mispereth, numbering; showing; increase of tribute

**Misrephoth-maim:** hot waters

**Mithcah:** sweetness; pleasantness

**Mithnite:** loin; gift; hope

**Mithredath:** breaking the law

**Mitylene:** purity; cleansing; press

**Mizar:** little

**Mizpah:** Mizpeh, a watch-tower; speculation

**Mizraim:** tribulations

**Mizzah:** defluxion from the head

**Mnason:** a diligent seeker; an exhorter

**Moab:** of his father

**Moladah:** birth; generation

**Molech:** Moloch, king

**Molid:** nativity; generation

**Mordecai:** contrition; bitter; bruising

**Moreh:** stretching

**Moriah:** bitterness of the Lord

**Moserah:** Moseroth, erudition; discipline

**Moses:** taken out; drawn forth

**Mozah:** unleavened

**Muppim:** out of the mouth; covering

**Mushi:** he that touches, that withdraws or takes away

**Myra:** I flow; pour out; weep

**Mysia:** criminal; abominable


**Naam:** fair; pleasant

**Naamah:** Naaman, beautiful; agreeable

**Naarah:** Naarai, young person

**Naashon:** that foretells; that conjectures

**Nabal:** fool; senseless

**Naboth:** words; prophecies

**Nachon:** ready; sure

**Nachor:** same as Nahor

**Nadab:** free and voluntary gift; prince

**Nagge:** clearness; brightness; light

**Nahaliel:** inheritance; valley of God

**Nahallal:** praised; bright

**Naham:** Nahamani, comforter; leader

**Naharai:** my nostrils; hot; anger

**Nahash:** snake; serpent

**Nahath:** rest; a leader

**Nahbi:** very secret

**Nahor:** hoarse; dry; hot

**Nahshon:** same as Naashon

**Nahum:** comforter; penitent

**Nain:** beauty; pleasantness

**Naioth:** beauties; habitations

**Naomi:** beautiful; agreeable

**Naphish:** the soul; he that rests, refreshes himself, or respires

**Naphtali:** that struggles or fights

**Narcissus:** astonishment; stupidity

**Nason:** helper; entry-way

**Nathan:** given; giving; rewarded

**Nathanael:** the gift of God

**Nathan-melech:** the gift of the king, or of counsel

**Naum:** same as Nahum

**Nazareth:** separated; crowned; sanctified

**Nazarite:** one chosen or set apart

**Neah:** moved; moving

**Neapolis:** the new city

**Neariah:** child of the Lord

**Nebai:** budding; speaking; prophesying

**Nebaioth:** words; prophecies; buds

**Neballat:** prophecy; budding

**Nebat:** that beholds

**Nebo:** that speaks or prophesies

**Nebuchadnezzar:** Nebuchadrezzar, tears and groans of judgment

**Nebushasi_hahban:** speech; prophecy; springing; flowing

**Nebuzar-adan:** fruits or prophecies of judgment

**Necho:** lame; beaten

**Nedabiah:** prince or vow of the Lord

**Neginoth:** stringed instruments

**Nehelamite:** dreamer; vale; brook

**Nehemiah:** consolation; repentance of the Lord

**Nehum:** comforter; penitent

**Nehushta:** made of brass

**Nehushtan:** a trifling thing of brass

**Neiel:** commotion, or moving, of God

**Nekoda:** painted; inconstant

**Nemuel:** the sleeping of God

**Nepheg:** weak; slacked

**Nephish:** same as Naphish

**Nephishesim:** diminished; torn in pieces

**Nephthalim:** same as Naphtali

**Nephthoah:** opening; open

**Nephusim:** same as Nephishesim

**Ner:** a lamp; new-tilled land

**Nereus:** same as Ner

**Nergal:** the great man; the hero

**Nergal-sharezer:** treasurer of Nergal

**Neri:** my light

**Neriah:** light; lamp of the Lord

**Nethaneel:** same as Nathanael

**Nethaniah:** the gift of the Lord

**Nethinims:** given or offered

**Neziah:** conqueror; strong

**Nezib:** standing-place

**Nibhaz:** budding; prophesying

**Nibshan:** prophecy; growing of a tooth

**Nicanor:** a conqueror; victorious

**Nicodemus:** victory of the people

**Nicolas:** same as Nicodemus

**Nicolaitanes:** followers of Nicolas

**Nicopolis:** the city of victory

**Niger:** black

**Nimrah:** Nimrim, leopard; bitterness; rebellion

**Nimrod:** rebellion (but probably an unknown Assyrian word)

**Nimshi:** rescued from danger

**Nineveh:** handsome; agreeable

**Nisan:** standard; miracle

**Nisroch:** flight; proof; temptation; delicate

**No:** stirring up; forbidding

**Noadiah:**  witness, or ornament, of the Lord

**Noah:**  repose; consolation

**Noah:**  that quavers or totters (Zelophehad's daughter)

**Nob:**  discourse; prophecy

**Nobah:**  that barks or yelps

**Nod:**  vagabond; fugitive

**Nodab:**  vowing of his own accord

**Noe:**  same as Noah

**Nogah:**  brightness; clearness

**Noha:**  rest; a guide

**Non:**  posterity; a fish; eternal

**Noph:**  honeycomb; anything that distills or drops

**Nophah:**  fearful; binding

**Nun:**  same as Non

**Nymphas:**  spouse; bridegroom


**Obadiah:**  servant of the Lord

**Obal:**  inconvenience of old age

**Obed:**  a servant; workman

**Obed-edom:**  servant of Edom

**Obil:**  that weeps; who deserves to be bewailed

**Oboth:** dragons; fathers; desires

**Ocran:** a disturber; that disorders

**Oded:** to sustain, hold or lift up

**Og:** a cake; bread baked in ashes

**Ohad:** praising; confessing

**Ohel:** tent; tabernacle; brightness

**Olympas:** heavenly

**Omar:** he that speaks; bitter

**Omega:** the last letter of the Greek alphabet; long O

**Omri:** sheaf of corn

**On:** pain; force; iniquity

**Onam:** Onan, same as On

**Onesimus:** profitable; useful

**Onesiphorus:** who brings profit

**Ono:** grief or strength or iniquity of him

**Ophel:** a tower; darkness; small white cloud

**Ophir:** fruitful region

**Ophni:** wearisomeness; folding together

**Ophrah:** dust; lead; a fawn

**Oreb:** a raven

**Ornan:** that rejoices

**Orpah:** the neck or skull

**Oshea:** same as Joshua

**Othni:** my time; my hour

**Othniel:** the hour of God

**Ozem:** that fasts; their eagerness

**Ozias:** strength from the Lord

**Ozni:** an ear; my hearkening

**Paarai:** opening

**Padan-aram:** cultivated field or table-land

**Padon:** his redemption; ox-yoke

**Pagiel:** prevention, or prayer, of God

**Pahath-Moab:** ruler of Moab

**Pai:** Pau, howling; sighing

**Palal:** thinking

**Palestina:** which is covered; watered; or brings and causes ruin

**Pallu:** marvelous; hidden

**Palti:** deliverance; flight

**Paltiel:** deliverance; or banishment, of God

**Pamphylia:** a nation made up of every tribe

**Paphos:** which boils, or is very hot

**Parah:** a cow; increasing

**Paran:** beauty; glory; ornament

**Parbar:** a suburb

**Parmashta:** a yearling bull

**Parmenas:** that abides, or is permanent

**Parnach:** a bull striking, or struck

**Parosh:** a flea; the fruit of a moth

**Parshandatha:** given by prayer

**Paruah:** flourishing; that flies away

**Pasach:** thy broken piece

**Pasdammin:** portion or diminishing of blood

**Paseah:** passing over; halting

**Pashur:** that extends or multiplies the hole; whiteness

**Patara:** trodden under foot

**Pathros:** Pathrusim, mouthful of dough; persuasion of ruin

**Patmos:** mortal

**Patrobas:** paternal; that pursues the steps of his father

**Pau:** same as Pai

**Paul:** small; little

**Paulus:** same as Paul

**Pedahzur:**  strong or powerful savior; stone of redemption

**Pedaiah:**  redemption of the Lord

**Pekah:**  he that opens; that is at liberty

**Pekahiah:**  it is the Lord that opens

**Pekod:**  noble; rulers

**Pelaiah:**  the Lord's secret or miracle

**Pelaliah:**  entreating the Lord

**Pelatiah:**  let the Lord deliver; deliverance of the Lord

**Peleg:**  division

**Pelethites:**  judges; destroyers

**Pelonite:**  falling; secret

**Peniel:**  face or vision of God; that sees God

**Peninnah:**  pearl; precious stone; the face

**Pentapolis:**  five cities

**Pentateuch:**  the five books of Moses

**Pentecost:**  fiftieth

**Penuel:**  same as Peniel

**Peor:**  hole; opening

**Perazim:**  divisions

**Peresh:**  horseman

**Perez:** divided

**Perez-Uzza:** division of Uzza, or of strength

**Perga:** very earthy

**Pergamos:** height; elevation

**Perida:** separation; division

**Perizzites:** dwelling in villages

**Persia:** that cuts or divides; a nail; a gryphon; a horseman

**Persis:** same as Persia

**Peruda:** same as Perida

**Peter:** a rock or stone

**Pethahiah:** the Lord opening; gate of the Lord

**Pethuel:** mouth of God; persuasion of God

**Peulthai:** my works

**Phalec:** same as Peleg

**Phallu:** Pallu, admirable; hidden

**Phalti Palti:** deliverance, flight

**Phanuel:** face or vision of God

**Pharaoh:** that disperses; that spoils

**Pharez:** division; rupture

**Pharisees:** set apart

**Pharpar:** that produces fruit

**Phebe:** shining; pure

**Phenice:** Phoenicia, red; purple

**Phichol:** the mouth of all, or every tongue

**Philadelphia:** love of a brother

**Philemon:** who kisses

**Philetus:** amiable; beloved

**Philip:** warlike; a lover of horses

**Philippi:** same as Philip, in the plural

**Philistines:** those who dwell in villages

**Philologus:** a lover of letters, or of the word

**Phinehas:** bold aspect; face of trust or protection

**Phlegon:** zealous; burning

**Phrygia:** dry; barren

**Phurah:** that bears fruit, or grows

**Phygellus:** fugitive

**Phylacteries:** things to be especially observed

**Pi-beseth:** abode of the goddess Bahest or Bast

**Pi-hahiroth:** the mouth; the pass of Hiroth

**Pilate:** armed with a dart

**Pinon:** pearl; gem; that beholds

**Piram:**  a wild ass of them

**Pirathon:**  his dissipation or deprivation; his rupture

**Pisgah:**  hill; eminence; fortress

**Pisidia:**  pitch; pitchy

**Pison:**  changing; extension of the mouth

**Pithom:**  their mouthful; a dilatation of the mouth

**Pithon:**  mouthful; persuasion

**Pochereth:**  cutting of the mouth of warfare

**Pontius:**  marine; belonging to the sea

**Pontus:**  the sea

**Poratha:**  fruitful

**Potiphar:**  bull of Africa; a fat bull

**Potipherah:**  that scatters abroad, or demolishes, the fat

**Prisca:**  ancient

**Priscilla:**  same as Prisca

**Prochorus:**  he that presides over the choirs

**Puah:**  mouth; corner; bush of hair

**Publius:**  common

**Pudens:**  shamefaced

**Pul:**  bean; destruction

**Punites:**  beholding; my face

**Punon:** precious stone; that beholds

**Pur:** Purim, lot

**Putiel:** God is my fatness

**Puteoli:** sulphureous wells

**Quartus:** fourth

**Raamah:** greatness; thunder; some sort of evil

**Raamiah:** thunder, or evil, from the Lord

**Rabbah:** great; powerful; contentious

**Rabbi:** Rabboni, my master

**Rabmag:** who overthrows or destroys a multitude

**Rab-saris:** chief of the eunuchs

**Rab-shakeh:** cup-bearer of the prince

**Raca:** worthless; good-for-nothing

**Rachab:** same as Rahab

**Rachal:** to whisper; an embalmer

**Rachel:** sheep

**Raddai:** ruling; coming down

**Ragau:** friend; shepherd

**Raguel:** shepherd, or friend of God

**Rahab:** proud; quarrelsome (applied to Egypt)

**Rahab:** large; extended (name of a woman)

**Raham:** compassion; a friend

**Rakkath:** empty; temple of the head

**Rakkon:** vain; void; mountain of enjoyment

**Ram:** elevated; sublime

**Ramah:** same as Ram

**Ramath:** Ramatha, raised; lofty

**Ramathaim-zophim:** the two watch-towers

**Ramath-lehi:** elevation of the jaw-bone

**Ramath-mizpeh:** elevation of the watch-tower

**Ramiah:** exaltation of the Lord

**Ramoth:** eminences; high places

**Raphah:** Raphu, relaxation; physic; comfort

**Reaiah:** vision of the Lord

**Reba:** the fourth; a square; that lies or stoops down

**Rebekah:** fat; fattened; a quarrel appeased

**Rechab:** square; chariot with team of four horses

**Reelaiah:** shepherd or companion to the Lord

**Regem:** that stones or is stoned; purple

**Regemmelech:** he that stones the king; purple of the king

**Rehabiah:** breadth, or extent, of the Lord

**Rehob:** breadth; space; extent

**Rehoboam:** who sets the people at liberty

**Rehoboth:** spaces; places

**Rehum:** merciful; compassionate

**Rei:** my shepherd; my companion; my friend

**Rekem:** vain pictures; divers picture

**Remaliah:** the exaltation of the Lord

**Remmon:** greatness; elevation; a pomegranate-tree

**Remphan:** prepared; arrayed

**Rephael:** the physic or medicine of God

**Rephaiah:** medicine or refreshment of the Lord

**Rehpaim:** giants; physicians; relaxed

**Rephidim:** beds; places of rest

**Resen:** a bridle or bit

**Reu:** his friend; his shepherd

**Reuben:** who sees the son; the vision of the son

**Reuel:** the shepherd or friend of God

**Reumah:** lofty; sublime

**Rezeph:** pavement; burning coal

**Rezin:** good-will; messenger

**Rezon:** lean; small; secret; prince

**Rhegium:** rupture; fracture

**Rhesa:** will; course

**Rhoda:** a rose

**Rhodes:** same as Rhoda

**Ribai:** strife

**Riblah:** quarrel; greatness to him

**Rimmon:** exalted; pomegranate

**Rinnah:** song; rejoicing

**Riphath:** remedy; medicine; release; pardon

**Rissah:** watering; distillation; dew

**Rithmah:** juniper; noise

**Rizpah:** bed; extension; a coal

**Rogelim:** a foot or footman

**Rohgah:** filled or drunk with talk

**Romamti-ezer:** exaltation of help

**Roman:** strong; powerful

**Rome:** strength; power

**Rosh:** the head; top, or beginning

**Rufus:** red

**Ruhamah:** having obtained mercy

**Rumah:** exalted; sublime; rejected

**Ruth:** drunk; satisfied

**Sabaoth:** Lord of hosts

**Sabeans:** captivity; conversion; old age

**Sabtah:** a going about or circuiting; old age

**Sabtechah:** that surrounds; that causes wounding

**Sacar:** wares; a price

**Sadducees:** followers of Sadoc, or Zadok

**Sadoc:** or Zadok, just; righteous

**Salah:** mission; sending

**Salamis:** shaken; test; beaten

**Salathiel:** asked or lent of God

**Salcah:** thy basket; thy lifting up

**Salem:** complete or perfect peace

**Salim:** foxes; fists; path

**Sallai:** Sallu, an exaltation; a basket

**Salma:** peace; perfection

**Salmon:** peaceable; perfect; he that rewards

**Salome:** same as Salmon

**Samaria:** watch-mountain

**Samlah:** his raiment; his left hand; his astonishment

**Samos:** full of gravel

**Samothracia:** an island possessed by the Samians and Thracians

**Samson:** his sun; his service; there the second time

**Samuel:** heard of God; asked of God

**Sanballat:** bramble-bush; enemy in secret

**Sanhedrin:** sitting together

**Sansannah:** bough or bramble of the enemy

**Saph:** rushes; sea-moss

**Saphir:** delightful

**Sapphira:** that relates or tells

**Sarah:** lady; princess; princess of the multitude

**Sarai:** my lady; my princess

**Sardis:** prince of joy

**Sardites:** removing a dissension

**Sarepta:** a goldsmith's shop

**Sargon:** who takes away protection

**Sarid:** remaining; hand of a prince

**Saron:** same as Sharon

**Sarsechim:** master of the wardrobe

**Saruch:** branch; layer; lining

**Satan:** contrary; adversary; enemy; accuser

**Saul:** demanded; lent; ditch; death

**Sceva:** disposed; prepared

**Seba:** a drunkard; that turns

**Sebat:** twig; scepter; tribe

**Secacah:** shadow; covering; defense

**Sechu:** defense; bough

**Secundus:** second

**Segub:** fortified; raised

**Seir:** Seirath, hairy; goat; demon; tempest

**Sela:** a rock

**Sela-hammah-lekoth:** rock of divisions

**Selah:** the end; a pause

**Seled:** affliction; warning

**Seleucia:** shaken or beaten by the waves

**Sem:** same as Shem

**Semachiah:** joined to the Lord

**Semaiah:** obeying the Lord

**Semei:** hearing; obeying

**Senaah:** bramble; enemy

**Seneh:** same as Senaah

**Senir:** bed-candle; changing

**Sennacherib:** bramble of destruction

**Seorim:** gates; hairs; tempests

**Sephar:** book; scribe; number

**Sepharad:** a book descending

**Sepharvaim:** the two books; the two scribes

**Serah:** lady of scent; song; the morning star

**Seraiah:** prince of the Lord

**Seraphim:** burning; fiery

**Sered:** dyer's vat

**Sergius:** net

**Serug:** branch; layer; twining

**Seth:** put; who puts; fixed

**Sethur:** hid; destroying

**Shaalabbim:** understanding, or son of a fox

**Shaalbim:** that beholds the heart

**Shaalbonite:** a fox's building

**Schaaph:** fleeing; thinking

**Shaaraim:** gates; valuation; hairs

**Shaashgaz:** he that presses the fleece; that shears the sheep

**Shabbethai:** my rest

**Shachia:** protection of the Lord

**Shadrach:** tender, nipple

**Shage:** touching softly; multiplying much

**Shalem:** same as Salem

**Shalim:** same as Salim

**Shalisha:** three; the third; prince; captain

**Shallum:** perfect; agreeable

**Shalmai:** my garment

**Shalman:** peaceable; perfect; that rewards

**Shalmaneser:** peace; tied; chained; perfection; retribution

**Shamariah:** throne or keeping of the Lord

**Shamed:** destroying; wearing out

**Shamer:** keeper; thorn; dregs

**Shamgar:** named a stranger; he is here a stranger

**Shamhuth:** desolation; destruction

**Shamir:** Shamer, prison; bush; lees; thorn

**Shammah:** loss; desolation; astonishment

**Shammai:** my name; my desolations

**Shammoth:** names; desolations

**Shammuah:** he that is heard; he that is obeyed

**Shamsherai:** there a singer or conqueror

**Shapham:** Shaphan, rabbit; wild rat; their lip; their brink

**Shaphat:** judge

**Sharai:** my lord; my prince; my song

**Sharar:** navel; thought; singing

**Sharezer:** overseer of the treasury, or of the storehouse

**Sharon:** his plain; his song

**Shashai:** rejoicing; mercy; linen

**Shashak:** a bag of linen; the sixth bag

**Shaul:** Saul, asked; lent; a grave

**Shaveh:** the plain; that makes equality

**Shealtiel:** same as Salathiel

**Sheariah:** gate of the Lord; tempest of the Lord

**Shear-jashub:** the remnant shall return

**Sheba:** captivity; old man; repose; oath

**Shebam:** compassing about; old men

**Shebaniah:** the Lord that converts, or recalls from captivity

**Shebarim:** breakings; hopes

**Sheber:** breaking; hope

**Shebna:** who rests himself; who is now captive

**Shebuel:** turning, or captivity, or seat, of God

**Shecaniah:** habitation of the Lord

**Shechem:** part; portion; back early in the morning

**Shedeur:** field of light; light of the Almighty

**Shehariah:** mourning or blackness of the Lord

**Shelah:** that breaks; that unties; that undresses

**Shelemiah:** God is my perfection; my happiness; my peace

**Sheleph:** who draws out

**Shelesh:** captain; prince

**Shelomi:** Shelomith, my peace; my happiness; my recompense

**Shelumiel:** same as Shelemiah

**Shem:** name; renown

**Shema:** hearing; obeying

**Shemaiah:** that hears or obeys the Lord

**Shemariah:** God is my guard

**Shemeber:** name of force; name of the strong

**Shemer:** guardian; thorn

**Shemida:** name of knowledge; that puts knowledge

**Sheminith:** eighth (an eight-stringed instrument)

**Shemiramoth:** the height of the heavens

**Shemuel:** appointed by God

**Shen:** tooth; ivory; change

**Shenazar:** treasurer of a tooth

**Shenir:** lantern; light that sleeps

**Shephatiah:** the Lord that judges

**Shephi:** beholder; honeycomb; garment

**Shepho:** desert

**Shephuphan:** serpent

**Sherah:** flesh; relationship

**Sherebiah:** singing with the Lord

**Sheshach:** bag of flax or linen

**Sheshai:** six; mercy; flax

**Sheshan:** lily; rose; joy; flax

**Sheshbazzar:** joy in tribulation; joy of the vintage

**Shethar:** putrefied; searching

**Shethar-boznai:** that makes to rot; that seeks those who despise me

**Sheva:** vanity; elevation; fame; tumult

**Shibboleth:** Sibboleth, ear of corn; stream or flood

**Shibmah:** overmuch captivity, or sitting

**Shicron:** drunkenness; his gift; his wages

**Shiggaion:** a song of trouble or comfort

**Shihon:** sound; wall of strength

**Shihor-libnah:** blackness of Libnah

**Shilhi:** Shilhim, bough; weapon; armor

**Shillem:** peace; perfection; retribution

**Shiloah:** same as Siloah

**Shiloh:** sent

**Shiloh (name of a city):** peace; abundance

**Shilom:** tarrying; peace-maker

**Shilshah:** three; chief; captain

**Shimeah:** Shimeath, that hears, or obeys; perdition

**Shimei:** Shimi, that hears or obeys; my reputation; my fame

**Shimeon:** same as Simeon

**Shimma:** same as Shimeah

**Shimon:** providing well; fatness; oil

**Shimrath:** hearing; obedient

**Shimshai:** my son

**Shimri:** thorn; dregs

**Shimrith:** Shimron, same as Shimri

**Shinab:** father of changing

113

**Shinar:** watch of him that sleeps

**Shiphi:** multitude

**Shiphrah:** handsome; trumpet; that does good

**Shisha:** of marble; pleasant

**Shishak:** present of the bag; of the pot; of the thigh

**Shitrai:** gatherer of money

**Shittim:** thorns

**Shiza:** this gift

**Shoa:** kings; tyrants

**Shobab:** returned; turned back; a spark

**Shobach:** your bonds; your chains

**Shobai:** turning captivity

**Shobal:** path; ear of corn

**Shobek:** made void; forsaken

**Shochoh:** defense; a bough

**Shoham:** keeping back

**Shomer:** keeper; dregs

**Shophach:** pouring out

**Shophan:** rabbit; hid

**Shoshannim:** those that shall be changed

**Shua:** crying; saving

**Shuah:** ditch; swimming; humiliation

**Shual:** fox; path; first

**Shubael:** returning captivity; seat of God

**Shuham:** talking; thinking; humiliation; budding

**Shulamite:** peaceable; perfect; that recompenses

**Shunem:** their change; their sleep

**Shuni:** changed; sleeping

**Shuphim:** Shuppim, wearing them out; their shore

**Shur:** wall; ox; that beholds

**Shushan:** lily; rose; joy

**Shuthelah:** plant; verdure; moist; pot

**Sia:** moving; help

**Sibbechai:** bough; cottage; of springs

**Sibmah:** conversion; captivity

**Sichem:** portion; shoulder

**Siddim:** the tilled field

**Sidon:** hunting; fishing; venison

**Sigionoth:** according to variable songs or tunes,

**Sihon:** rooting out; conclusion

**Sihor:** black; trouble (the river Nile)

115

**Silas:** three, or the third

**Silla:** exalting

**Siloa:** Siloam, Siloe, same as Shilhi

**Silvanus:** who loves the forest

**Simeon:** that hears or obeys; that is heard

**Simon:** that hears; that obeys

**Sin:** bush

**Sinai:** a bush; enmity

**Sinim:** south country,

**Sion:** noise; tumult

**Sippai:** threshold; silver cup

**Sinon:** a breast-plate; deliverance

**Sisamai:** house; blindness

**Sisera:** that sees a horse or a swallow

**Sitnah:** hatred

**Sivan:** a bush or thorn

**Smyrna:** myrrh

**So:** a measure for grain; vail

**Socoh:** tents; tabernacles

**Sodi:** my secret

**Sodom:** their secret; their cement

**Solomon:** peaceable; perfect; one who recompenses

**Sopater:** Sosipater, who defends the father

**Sophereth:** scribe, numbering

**Sorek:** vine; hissing; a color inclining to yellow

**Sosthenes:** savior; strong; powerful

**Sotai:** conclusion in pleading; binding

**Spain:** rare; precious

**Stachys:** spike or ear of corn

**Stephanas:** crown; crowned

**Stephen:** same as Stephanas

**Suah:** speaking; entreating; ditch

**Succoth:** tents; tabernacles

**Succoth-benoth:** the tents of daughters, or young women; or prostitutes

**Sud:** my secret

**Sur:** that withdraws or departs; rebellion

**Susanna:** lily; rose; joy

**Susi:** horse; swallow; moth

**Sychar:** end

**Syene:** a bush; enmity

**Syntyche:** that speaks or discourses

**Syracuse:** that draws violently


**Taanach:** who humbles thee; who answers thee

**Taanach-shilo:** breaking down a fig-tree

**Tabbath:** good; goodness

**Tabeal:** Tabeel, good God

**Taberah:** burning

**Tabitha:** clear-sighted; a roe-deer

**Tabor:** choice; purity; bruising

**Tabrimon:** good pomegranate; the navel; the middle

**Tadmor:** the palm-tree; bitterness

**Tahan:** beseeching; merciful

**Tahapenes:** secret temptation

**Tahath:** fear; going down

**Tahpenes:** standard; flight; temptation

**Tahrea:** anger; wicked contention

**Talitha-cumi:** young woman, arise

**Talmai:** my furrow; that suspends the waters; heap of waters

**Tamah:** blotting or wiping out; smiting

**Tamar:** palm; palm-tree

**Tammuz:** abstruse; concealed; consumed

**Tanach:** same as Taanach

**Tanhumeth:** consolation; repentance

**Taphath:** distillation; drop

**Tappuah:** apple; swelling

**Tarah:** a hair; a wretch; one banished

**Taralah:** searching out slander, or strength

**Tarea:** howling; doing evil

**Tarpelites:** ravishers; succession of miracles

**Tarshish:** contemplation; examination

**Tarsus:** winged; feathered

**Tartak:** chained; bound; shut up

**Tartan:** a general (official title)

**Tatnai:** that gives; the overseer of the gifts and tributes

**Tebah:** murder; butchery; guarding of the body; a cook

**Tebaliah:** baptism, or goodness, of the Lord

**Tebeth:** good, goodness (the tenth month of the Hebrews)

**Tehinnah:** entreaty; a favor

**Tekel:** weight

**Tekoa:** trumpet; that is confirmed

**Telabib:** a heap of new grain

**Telah:** moistening; greenness

**Telassar:** taking away; heaping up

**Telem:** their dew; their shadow

**Telharsa:** suspension of the plow

**Tel-melah:** heap of salt

**Tema:** admiration; perfection; consummation

**Teman:** Temani, the south; Africa; perfect

**Terah:** to breathe; scent; blow

**Teraphim:** images; idols

**Tertius:** third

**Tertullus:** third

**Tetrarch:** governor of a fourth part

**Thaddeus:** that praises or confesses

**Thahash:** that makes haste; that keeps silence

**Thamah:** that blots out; that suppresses

**Tharah:** same as Terah

**Thebez:** muddy; eggs; fine linen or silk

**Thelasar:** same as Telassar

**Theophilus:** friend of God

**Thessalonica:** victory against the Thessalians

**Theudas:** flowing with water

**Thomas:** a twin

**Thummim:** perfection; truth

**Thyatira:** a perfume; sacrifice of labor

**Tibbath:** killing; a cook

**Tiberias:** good vision; the navel

**Tiberius:** the son of Tiber

**Tibni:** straw; hay

**Tidal:** that breaks the yoke; knowledge of elevation

**Tiglath-pileser:** that binds or takes away captivity

**Tikvah:** hope; a little line; congregation

**Tilon:** murmuring

**Timeus:** perfect; admirable; honorable

**Timnah:** forbidding

**Timnath:** image; figure; enumeration

**Timnath-heres:** or Timnath-serah, image of the sun; numbering of the rest

**Timon:** honorable; worthy

**Timotheus:** honor of God; valued of God

**Tiphsah:** passage; leap; step; the passover

**Tirhakah:** inquirer; examiner; dull observer

**Tiria:** searching out

**Tirshatha:** a governor

**Tirzah:** benevolent; complaisant; pleasing

**Tishbite:** that makes captive

**Titus:** pleasing

**Toah:** weapon; dart

**Tob:** good; goodness

**Tob-adonijah:** my good God; the goodness of the foundation of the Lord

**Tobiah:** Tobijah, the Lord is good

**Tochen:** middle

**Togarmah:** which is all bone

**Tohu:** that lives; that declares

**Toi:** who wanders

**Tola:** worm; grub; scarlet

**Tolad:** a generation

**Tophel:** ruin; folly; without understanding

**Tophet:** a drum; betraying

**Trachonitis:** stony

**Troas:** penetrated

**Trophimus:** well educated; well brought up

**Tryphena:** delicious; delicate

**Tryphon:** masculine of Tryphena

**Tryphosa:** thrice shining

**Tubal:** the earth; the world; confusion

**Tubal-cain:** worldly possession; possessed of confusion

**Tychicus:** casual; by chance

**Tyrannus:** a prince; one that reigns

**Tyre:** Tyrus, strength; rock; sharp

**Ucal:** power, prevalency

**Uel:** desiring God

**Ulai:** strength; fool; senseless

**Ulam:** the porch; the court; their strength; their folly

**Ulla:** elevation; leaf; young child

**Ummah:** darkened; covered; his people

**Unni:** poor; afflicted; that answers

**Uphaz:** pure gold; gold of Phasis or Pison

**Upharsin:** divided

**Ur:** fire, light, a valley

**Urbane:** courteous

**Uri:** my light, my fire

**Uriah:** or Urijah, the Lord is my light or fire

**Uriel:** same as Uriah

**Urim:** lights; fires

**Uthai:** my iniquity

**Uz:** counsel; words

**Uzai:** he

**Uzal:** wandering

**Uzzah:** strength; goat

**Uzzen-sherah:** ear of the flesh

**Uzzi:** my strength; my kid

**Uzziah:** Uzziel, the strength, or kid, of the Lord

**Vajezatha:** sprinkling the chamber

**Vaniah:** nourishment, or weapons, of the Lord

**Vashni:** the second; changed; a tooth

**Vashti:** that drinks; thread

**Vophsi:** fragrant; diminution

**There are no entries for W.**

**There are no entries for X.**

**There are no entries for Y.**

**Zaanannim:** movings; a person asleep

**Zaavan:** trembling

**Zabad:** dowry; endowed

**Zabbai:** flowing

**Zabdi:** same as Zabad

**Zaccai:** pure meat; just

**Zaccheus:** pure; clean; just

**Zaccur:** of the male kind; mindful

**Zachariah:** memory of the Lord

**Zadok:** just; justified

**Zaham:** crime; filthiness; impurity

**Zair:** little; afflicted; in tribulation

**Zalaph:** shadow; ringing; shaking

**Zalmon:** his shade; his image

**Zalmonah:** the shade; the sound of the number; his image

**Zalmunna:** shadow; image; idol forbidden

**Zamzummims:** projects of crimes; enormous crimes

**Zanoah:** forgetfulness; desertion

**Zaphnath-paaneah:** one who discovers hidden things

**Zarah:** east; brightness

**Zareah:** leprosy; hornet

**Zared:** strange descent

**Zarephath:** ambush of the mouth

**Zaretan:** tribulation; perplexity

**Zatthu:** olive tree

**Zaza:** belonging to all

**Zebadiah:** portion of the Lord; the Lord is my portion

**Zebah:** victim; sacrifice

**Zebedee:** abundant; portion

**Zebina:** flowing now; selling; buying

**Zeboiim:** deer; goats

**Zebudah:** endowed; endowing

**Zebul:** a habitation

**Zebulun:** Zebulon, dwelling; habitation

**Zechariah:** same as Zachariah

**Zedad:** his side; his hunting

**Zedekiah:** the Lord is my justice; the justice of the Lord

**Zeeb:** wolf

**Zelah:** rib; side; halting

**Zelek:** the shadow or noise of him that licks or laps

**Zelophehad:** the shade or tingling of fear

**Zelotes:** zealous

**Zelzah:** noontide

**Zemaraim:** wool; pith

**Zemira:** song; vine; palm

**Zenan:** coldness; target; weapon

**Zenas:** living

**Zephaniah:** the Lord is my secret

**Zephath:** which beholds; that attends or that covers

**Zepho:** Zephon, that sees and observes; that expects or covers

**Zer:** perplexity

**Zerah:** same as Zarah

**Zerahiah:** the Lord rising; brightness of the Lord

**Zeredah:** ambush; change of dominion

**Zeresh:** misery; strange; dispersed inheritance

**Zereth:** same as Zer

**Zeror:** root; that straitens or binds; that keeps tight

**Zeruah:** leprous; wasp; hornet

**Zerubbabel:** a stranger at Babylon; dispersion of confusion

**Zeruiah:** pain or tribulation of the Lord

**Zethar:** he that examines or beholds

**Zia:** sweat; swelling

**Ziba:** army; fight; strength

**Zibeon:**  iniquity that dwells

**Zibiah:**  the Lord dwells; deer; goat

**Zichri:**  that remembers; that is a man

**Ziddim:**  huntings; treasons; destructions

**Zidkijah:**  justice of the Lord

**Zidon:**  hunting; fishing; venison

**Zif:**  this or that; brightness; comeliness

**Ziha:**  brightness; whiteness; drought

**Ziklag:**  measure pressed down

**Zillah:**  shadow; the tingling of the ear

**Zilpah:**  distillation from the mouth

**Zilthai:**  my shadow; my talk

**Zimmah:**  thought; wickedness

**Zimran:**  song; singer; vine

**Zimzi:**  my field; my vine

**Zin:**  buckler; coldness

**Zina:**  shining; going back

**Zion:**  monument; raised up; sepulcher

**Zior:**  ship of him that watches

**Ziph:**  this mouth or mouthful; falsehood

**Ziphron:** falsehood of a song; rejoicing

**Zippor:** bird; sparrow; crown; desert

**Zipporah:** beauty; trumpet; mourning

**Zithri:** to hide; demolished

**Ziz:** flower; branch; a lock of hair

**Ziza:** same as Zina

**Zoan:** motion

**Zoar:** little; small

**Zobah:** Zobebah, an army; warring

**Zohar:** white; bright; dryness

**Zoheleth:** that creeps, slides, or draws

**Zoheth:** separation; amazing

**Zophah:** viol; honeycomb

**Zophar:** rising early; crown

**Zophim:** place for a watchman

**Zorah:** leprosy; scab; hornet

**Zorobabel:** same as Zerubbabel

**Zuar:** same as Zoar

**Zuph:** that beholds, observes, watches; roof; covering

**Zur:** stone; rock; that besieges

**Zuriel:** rock or strength of God

**Zurishaddai:**  the Almighty is my rock and strength

**Zuzims:**  the posts of a door; splendor; beauty

*Also from Benediction Books ...*
**Wandering Between Two Worlds: Essays on Faith and Art**
**Anita Mathias**
Benediction Books, 2007
152 pages
ISBN: 0955373700

Available from www.amazon.com, www.amazon.co.uk

In these wide-ranging lyrical essays, Anita Mathias writes, in lush, lovely prose, of her naughty Catholic childhood in Jamshedpur, India; her large, eccentric family in Mangalore, a sea-coast town converted by the Portuguese in the sixteenth century; her rebellion and atheism as a teenager in her Himalayan boarding school, run by German missionary nuns, St. Mary's Convent, Nainital; and her abrupt religious conversion after which she entered Mother Teresa's convent in Calcutta as a novice. Later rich, elegant essays explore the dualities of her life as a writer, mother, and Christian in the United States-- Domesticity and Art, Writing and Prayer, and the experience of being "an alien and stranger" as an immigrant in America, sensing the need for roots.

**About the Author**

Anita Mathias was born in India, has a B.A. and M.A. in English from Somerville College, Oxford University and an M.A. in Creative Writing from the Ohio State University. Her essays have been published in The Washington Post, The London Magazine, The Virginia Quarterly Review, Commonweal, Notre Dame Magazine, America, The Christian Century, Religion Online, The Southwest Review, Contemporary Literary Criticism, New Letters, The Journal, and two of HarperSanFrancisco's The Best Spiritual Writing anthologies. Her non-fiction has won fellowships from The National Endowment for the Arts; The Minnesota State Arts Board; The Jerome Foundation, The Vermont Studio Center; The Virginia Centre for the Creative Arts, and the First Prize for the Best General Interest Article from the Catholic Press Association of the United States and Canada. Anita has taught Creative Writing at the College of William and Mary, and now lives and writes in Oxford, England.

www.anitamathias.com,
christiancogitations.blogspot.com
wanderingbetweentwoworlds.blogspot.com

www.ingramcontent.com/pod-product-compliance
Lightning Source LLC
Chambersburg PA
CBHW030519100426

42813CB00001B/94